AF781609

JUSTICE IN ISLAM

NEW ETHICAL PERSPECTIVES

JUSTICE IN ISLAM

NEW ETHICAL PERSPECTIVES

Edited by

RAMON HARVEY AND DANIEL TUTT

INTERNATIONAL INSTITUTE OF ISLAMIC THOUGHT

© The International Institute of Islamic Thought, 1444 AH/2023 CE

IIIT, P.O. Box 669, Herndon, VA 20172, USA
www.iiit.org

London Office
P.O. Box 126, Richmond, Surrey TW9 2UD, UK
www.iiituk.com

This book is in copyright.Subject to statutory exception and to the provisions of relevant collective licensing agreements, no reproduction of any part may take place without the written permission of the publisher

TITLE: JUSTICE IN ISLAM: NEW ETHICAL PERSPECTIVES
EDITORS: RAMON HARVEY AND DANIEL TUTT

ISBN 978-1-64205-657-0 paperback
ISBN 978-1-64205-656-3 hardback
ISBN 978-1-64205-658-7 eBook

The views and opinions expressed in this book are those of the contributors and not necessarily those of the publisher. The publisher is not responsible for the accuracy of URLs for external or third-party internet websites referred to in this publication, and does not guarantee that any content on such websites is, or will remain, accurate or appropriate

Typesetting and cover design by Shiraz Khan

Printed in USA

CONTENTS

CONTRIBUTORS

Monir Birouk (Assistant Professor, Ibn Zohr University) specializes in contemporary Arab-Islamic philosophical thought with a focus on the dialectic between modernity and ethics in the thought of the Moroccan philosopher Taha Abderrahmane. He earned his doctorate from Mohamed V University in Rabat, Morocco.

Philip Dorroll (Associate Professor of Religion, Wofford College) works in the history of Islamic theology in classical Arabic and Modern Turkish. He also conducts comparative studies of Eastern Christian and Islamic theology. His current projects include the history of Māturīdite *kalām* and the development of a model for comparative theologies of modern Orthodox Christianity and Sunnī Islam. He received his doctorate from Emory University.

Samaneh Oladi Ghadikolaei (Assistant Professor of Religious Studies, Virginia Commonwealth University) specializes in Islamic jurisprudence, family law, and women's studies. Her current research looks at the evolving roles of women as religious authorities and producers of Islamic knowledge, addressing how their scholarship challenges patriarchal interpretations of sacred scriptures. She is working on a book that looks at Muslim women's religious activism and its impact on bridging the gap between Islamic jurisprudence and gender justice. She received her doctorate from the University of California, Santa Barbara.

Ramon Harvey (Aziz Foundation Lecturer in Islamic Studies, Cambridge Muslim College) works in the fields of Qur'anic studies, theology, and ethics, both as an intellectual historian and theologian. He is the author of *The Qur'an and the Just Society* (2018) and *Transcendent God, Rational World: A Māturīdī Theology* (2021), which are published by Edinburgh University Press. He is also the editor of the monograph series *Edinburgh Studies in Islamic Scripture and Theology*. He earned his doctorate from SOAS, University of London.

Xiaofei Tu (Assistant Professor, Department of Languages, Literatures, and Cultures, Appalachian State University) specializes in contemporary East Asian philosophy, including Chinese Islamic thought. A 2012 U.S. Department of State cultural exchange grant recipient, he is working on a book on Asian popular culture and nationalism, in which he explores the possibility for transnational pop culture to break down national boundaries and bring people in Asia together. He earned his master's and doctorate degrees from Harvard and Syracuse Universities.

Daniel Tutt (Lecturer in Philosophy, George Washington University) works on continental philosophy, contemporary social and political movements, Islamic thought and psychoanalysis. His forthcoming book is entitled *Psychoanalysis and the Politics of the Family: The Crisis of Initiation* and will be published in the Palgrave Lacan Series in 2022. His writing has been published in *Philosophy Now, The Islamic Monthly* and *Crisis and Critique*, among other publications. He teaches philosophy at George Washington University, Marymount University and has taught inmates through the Georgetown University Prisons and Justice Initiative.

FOREWORD

The IIIT is pleased to present this important work, *Justice in Islam: New Ethical Perspectives*. Justice is not solely the preserve of scholarly theories but an ethical responsibility encumbent upon us all, and a fundamental principle for the healthy functioning of societies. It has real-world implications, which can either cause great happiness or great misery and oppression. As such justice has been at the heart of much religious and moral philosophical discourse across the centuries: where there is loss of justice, nothing is left but suffering in its wake. And because we are all so intrinsically invested in its correct implementation, the beliefs people hold act as a powerful framework upon which to establish justice, whether in the institutions society chooses to set up for itself or the level of political governance. Yet old notions are having to pave way for new as traditional perspectives on ethics and morality are rapidly shifting with gender, for instance, at the forefront of the human-rights debate. As those traditional virtues erode, and hitherto, centuries-old shared understandings of ethics disintegrate, ever more new complex challenges arise that need addressing. Furthermore, we are witnessing unparalleled levels of wealth and inequality, with billionaires on one side and extreme poverty on the other, and with everyone unsure as to where accountability goes, or how to even fathom the intricacies of the economics that undergirds it. As such, the subject of justice is gaining greater significance and urgency in the modern context with societies, in the face of mounting levels of inequality (whatever their form), searching for ways to solve the many problems arising.

For Muslims, ethical understandings and justice are bound up with the Qur'an and Prophetic Sunnah, never to be detached from the real world or from God, and certainly not the preserve of shifting human opinion or sentiments of the day. Utilising Islamic principles of ethics to enact justice in today's world requires making sense of that world as never before. Muslims need to understand the modern age, to think through how best to realize obligations of justice in contemporary times and be careful of compromises. Thus ethical questions need to be explored with perspectives examined to address the various complex challenges facing Islam from differing directions in this regard, and the solutions it offers.

This book discusses various conceptions of justice and the underlying moral foundations and principles of the Islamic perspective governing understanding, pushing further the boundaries of dialogue and critical analysis. Written in a clear and lucid style, it is hoped it will benefit both general and specialist readers alike, increasing their awareness of the issues raised as well as exploring modern scholarly discourse on the subject.

Since its establishment in 1981, the IIIT has served as a major center to facilitate serious scholarly efforts. Towards this end it has, over the decades, conducted numerous programs of research, seminars, and conferences as well as publishing scholarly works specializing in the social sciences and areas of theology, which to date number more than six hundred titles in English and Arabic, many of which have been translated into other major languages.

We would like to thank Dr. Ramon Harvey and Dr. Daniel Tutt for their editorial work and cooperation throughout the various stages of production, as well as the contributors, and all those who were directly or indirectly involved in the completion of this book. May God reward them for their efforts.

IIIT

MARCH 2023

Mapping Justice in Islamic Thought: From the Premodern to the Postmodern

Ramon Harvey and Daniel Tutt

> We see neither justice nor injustice which does not change its nature with change in climate. Three degrees of latitude reverse all jurisprudence; a meridian decides the truth...A strange justice that is bounded by a river!
> ***Blaise Pascal*** (1623-62)[1]

If one were to pick a single unifying ethical theme for the history of Islamic thought, a good case could be made for justice. Easy to claim, hard to define, justice is an ever-present concern in the warp and weft of Muslim societies and their intellectual articulations. In the current era, the question of justice in Islam, whether affirmed or critiqued, is not just contemplated by Muslims but engages scholars and the public all over the world. There is a real need for contemporary scholarship to understand where this discussion is heading in its diverse, global dimensions. This volume seeks to contribute to mapping this terrain, but to explain how we think it can do this, it is necessary to explore the genealogy of the question of justice in Islam. We can only understand what the present moment means and what may come if we can adequately relate it to the past.

In this introductory essay, we aim to track the discourse of justice within key moments of Islamic history. What emerges is a lively story punctuated by epistemic debates over the status of universality, the ethical underpinnings and proper place of justice within a given society, and the role of the state in its administration. These debates occur within scholarly communities and are shaped by engagement with traditions and philosophies of justice that Muslim scholars came into contact with from the earliest stages in Islamic history. Despite this, by no means is the discourse of justice in Islam exclusively housed within the scholarly community. Rather, from its first developments within Islamic thought, it has been forged in confrontation and dialogue with a multitude of theological and philosophical movements.

The perspectives on justice that we track in this introduction are driven by a commitment to preserving the wider truths of revelation and its subsequent interpretive authorities, all the while responding to changing social and political realities. The ethical dimension of this genealogy is thus a touchstone in presenting the normative basis of ideals, virtues and models for the achievement of justice. Yet the political haunts and provokes the ethical at every juncture, pushing it to challenge, modify and reform its presuppositions.

Premodern Islamic Thought: Threads of Justice

Ibn Isḥāq (d. 150/767), the early compiler of the biography of the Prophet Muhammad, documents a famous pact that the Prophet witnessed when he was young, the *ḥilf al-fuḍūl* (the pact of the "excess").[2] His clan of Hāshim, along with other factions of his tribe, Quraysh, gathered together and promised to stand by both the oppressed among themselves and others who entered Makkah. Anyone who had kept an excess portion of goods would not be left alone until they had returned what was due. Ibn Isḥāq quotes the Prophet as follows: "I witnessed in the house of ʿAbd Allāh b. Judʿān a pact more beloved to me than red camels. Were I called to [honor] it in Islam, I would respond to it."[3]

A Muslim seeking to uphold justice in the same way today may look to the Prophet's (ṢAAS)* revealed book for guidance, though the Qur'an nowhere defines the concept. The Arabic recitation that spilled into history from the Prophet's lips implicitly assumes that its audience already knows the basics of right and wrong, as the story of the *ḥilf al-fuḍūl* illustrates.[4] The Qur'an's immediate moral function, then, is as a reminder and call to reform for an Arabian society that had become degraded and lost its way. At the same time, the Qur'an speaks with a broader voice as the culminating revelation in a series of divine dispensations since the dawn of time.[5] These two aspects intersect in the following passage:

> If they reject you [Prophet], so did the people of Noah before them, and those of 'Ad, Thamud, Abraham, Lot, Midian. Moses too was called a liar. I gave the unfaithful time, but in the end I punished them. How I condemned them! How many towns steeped in wrongdoing We have destroyed and left in total ruin; how many deserted wells; how many lofty palaces! Have these people [of Makkah] not travelled through the land with hearts to understand and ears to

*(ṢAAS – *Ṣallā Allāhu ʿalayhi wa sallam.* May the peace and blessings of God be upon him. Said whenever the name of Prophet Muhammad is mentioned).

> hear? It is not people's eyes that are blind, but their hearts within their breasts (22:42-6).[6]

That the corruption of society, and even the destruction of nations, is something brought upon people by their own injustices becomes a principle of divine regulation of the world: "Corruption has flourished on land and sea as a result of people's actions and He will make them taste the consequences of some of their own actions so that they may turn back (30:41)"; "God would never change a favor He had conferred on a people unless they changed what was within themselves. God is all hearing, all knowing (8:53)." The interrelationship between individual, society and God is an important motif for justice in the Qur'an and in Islam. The action of each implies the response of the other and so to study any one in isolation would distort the resultant conception.

Analogously, the philosopher Charles Taylor has used the term "porous self" to describe the way in which within premodern Christian thought meanings arising from an "enchanted world" interpenetrate with individual subjectivities. He contrasts this with the modern "buffered self" that sees the world as a separated external entity.[7] Have modern Islamic ideas of justice lost the holistic perspective available at the time of the scripture's revelation? Is this in any case inevitable? The least that we can do is to try to account for those differences in intellectual framing that may have emerged over time. Identifying such gaps may even give us the theoretical space to critique contemporary Muslim accounts of justice and to construct new articulations to overcome the identified shortcomings.

A first step is to trace, however partially, the history of ideas relevant to justice within Muslim theological and ethico-legal traditions. Before getting to such discursive formations, we must assess their political dimensions within the earliest period. While the Qur'an does speak in political terms, especially in its affirmation of the governance role that the Prophet Muhammad holds over the community of believers, it does not lay down generally applicable injunctions in this sphere. Rather, it draws from the sacred history of previous prophetic communities to provide specific guidance for the situations faced by the early Muslims in Makkah and Madinah.[8]

Likewise, the Qur'an provides no blueprint for the community's political or leadership following the death of the Prophet.[9] This gave space for the emergence of competing narratives of political justice within the formative period of Islam. A tendency within Muslim thought that would later be expressed as Sunnism emphasised the justice of the first four "rightly guided" caliphs, especially the key legal and governance decisions made by the second caliph, ʿUmar b. al-Khaṭṭāb. From the alternative perspective of nascent Shiʿism, true justice was embodied by the Prophet's cousin, the fourth caliph, ʿAlī b. Abī Ṭālib, who, it was believed, should have succeeded him instead of Abū Bakr.

The discourse of caliphal legitimacy retained a potent connection to that of justice in the early centuries of Islam, especially in connection to repeated rebellions against the Umayyad dynasty and its eventual fall to the Abbasids. Over time, however, the idea of justice transcended its concrete expression in politics, increasingly becoming a subject for theological and ethical deliberation and a rallying cry for pious and upright social conduct. In this vein, the early Kufan theologian and jurist Abū Ḥanīfah (d. 150/767) used the name the People of Justice and the People of Precedent (*ahl al-ʿadl wa al-ahl al-sunnah*), in a letter defending the correctness of his theological beliefs.[10] This usage reflected social activism in the form of the Qur'anic principle of "enjoining good and forbidding evil (*al-amr bi al-maʿrūf wa al-nahy ʿan al-munkar*)",[11] which was adopted as a slogan in the early centuries by many groups and movements with varying ideas of how it was best to be carried out.[12]

One of the most famous groups to adopt the language of justice was the Muʿtazilites, a theological school sometimes closely associated with Ḥanafism that emerged from the beginning of the third/ninth century and drew from various sources including the Hellenic legacy to take a specific set of rationalistic approaches to questions of theology and scriptural interpretation. The Muʿtazilites dubbed themselves the People of Justice and Unicity (*ahl al-ʿadl wa al-tawḥīd*), though the word *ʿadl* in this expression reflected for them a particular way of understanding God's justice in terms of human ethical intuitions.[13] Many doctrines of the Muʿtazilites were considered problematic within the emerging contours of Sunnite thought, though their focus on justice was picked up by both Zaydite and Imāmite Shiʿite traditions as a way of expressing a theology that put center stage the unjust martyring of charismatic leaders from the Prophet's family.[14] The ideas of Abū Ḥanīfah, on the other hand, found their most fruitful continuation in the work of the Transoxianan theologian Abū Manṣūr al-Māturīdī (d. 333/944). He provided an alternative articulation of scriptural and rational sources that highlighted the importance of God's eternal wisdom (*ḥikmah*) as the basis of His justice.[15]

A different set of emphases on justice can be found in the fifth/eleventh century Ashᶜarite theologian and Sufi Abū Ḥāmid al-Ghazālī (d. 505/1111) who is acclaimed for his influential synthesis of traditional and philosophical modes of thought, especially reception of the ideas of Ibn Sīnā (Avicenna) (d. 429/1037). An interesting example is furnished by the twentieth chapter of his magnum opus *The Revival of the Disciplines of Religion (Iḥyā ᶜulūm al-dīn)*, which is entitled "The Chapter of the Manners of Living and Prophetic Character (*Kitāb ādāb al-maᶜīshah wa akhlāq al-nubuwwah*)". He describes the Prophet Muhammad as "the most prudent (*aḥlam*), courageous (*ashjaᶜ*), just (*aᶜdal*) and temperant (*aᶜaff*) of people".[16] Though these qualities can be individually traced back to hadiths,[17] the manner in which al-Ghazālī combines them is ultimately derived from the four cardinal virtues in Plato's *Republic*. Within Plato's framework, justice is the master virtue that regulates the other three qualities in both the macrocosm of the ideal society, and the microcosm of the virtuous person.[18] For al-Ghazālī, the Prophet's justice, an exemplar affirmed through tradition, can be mapped onto the ethical framework handed down by Hellenic thought.

A reaction to al-Ghazālī's Hellenizing endeavour is present in the oeuvre of the reformist Damascene theologian Ibn Taymiyyah (d. 728/1328) who put great stress on the human natural disposition (*fiṭrah*) for moral knowledge and its consonance with revealed codes. Ovamir Anjum argues that living at the tail end of the Crusades and Mongol conquests, Ibn Taymiyyah was concerned by what he saw as the corruption of Muslim understanding and practice that must be held responsible for the collapse of traditional Islamic political strength.[19] Rather than putting the categories of the philosophical tradition into conversation with revelation, Ibn Taymiyyah used rational argument to support a pietist return to the basic concepts of scripture, while using his considerable erudition to forge a new theological perspective that placed the political and legal aspects of justice at its forefront.[20]

In the late classical and early modern eras, the emergence within the Muslim world of three major empires became highly significant to the further development of intellectual culture, including discourses of justice. The Ottoman, Safavid and Mughal empires all developed in power and influence during the ninth/fifteenth and tenth/sixteenth centuries. To a certain extent, this period saw the reintegration of political power and the legal ideal of justice in a way that had been dormant within the prior tradition.

The preeminent Sunnite Ottoman jurist, Abū al-Suᶜūd (d. 982/1574), articulated a new role for the Ottoman sultan as a universal caliph with the responsibility to establish God's law on earth. This bold theological-cum-jurisprudential move enabled him to give Sultan Suleiman the Manificent (d. 974/1566) an instrumental role as a point of reference in the interpretation of the Shariᶜah and religiously validated his decrees as part of the regime of divine justice in the world.[21] The magnification of the sultan's legal authority did not, however, break the long-established condition that the ruler was subject to the Shariᶜah like any other private citizen and could, in theory at least, be brought by the ulema in front of a court for any claimed infraction.[22]

A parallel development occurred in the rival Safavid Empire. For the Imāmite Shiᶜites, the true imam was in occultation, awaited as the future Mahdī. Political authority thus began to become invested in the person of the just jurist. Although this idea was already implicit in the works of earlier figures, it advanced due to the thought of al-Muḥaqqiq al-Karakī (d. 941/1534) and other Safavid jurists.[23] This set the stage for the modern development of political Shiᶜism.

A more ambitious reform of Muslim socio-political thought was attempted by the late-Mughal Indian scholar Shāh Walī Allāh al-Dahlawī (d. 1186/1762) who attempted a grand synthesis of the Islamic tradition. His thinking on the development of society sought to stitch together many of the intellectual strands available to him, including the ideas of Ibn Taymiyyah, Neoplatonic Muslim philosophers such as al-Fārābī (d. 339/950-51) and others. In the area of social justice, he added a sophisticated appreciation of its economic dimensions, a contribution that proved influential in twentieth-century Muslim thought.[24]

Whereas the trajectories highlighted so far represent important intra-Muslim debates that continue to the present day, the emergence of Western European nations as colonial powers in the nineteenth century and its aftermath upended Muslim discussions of justice. For the first time, Islam as an intellectual tradition has been compelled to grapple with the ideas of the West from a position of weakness not strength. Therefore understanding the challenges that this situation poses remains of central importance to anyone interrogating the contemporary question of justice in Islam.

The Colonial Period: Upheaval and Reform

The colonial period, symbolically marked by Napoleon's invasion of Egypt in 1798, transformed the shape of Muslim societies. The presence of the European colonial powers throughout the Middle East, North Africa and the Far East would create the circumstances for oppression and exploitation but also the rebirth of innovative thinking around justice. In the face of profound intellectual, social and political instability, new trajectories of thought influenced struggles for liberation and freedom.

Whereas the precolonial period can be characterized as an era in which rulers of Muslim polities relied on a largely autonomous network of qadis to implement the Shariʿah and civil law (*qānūn*) in communal and civil courts, the colonial period witnessed the breakdown of this system. Muslim citizens could no longer rely on an Islamic jurisprudential model to dispense justice within their lives. It was not only colonialism that disrupted the political and ethical dynamics of Muslim societies. The emergence of the capitalist world system; the formation of nation states; the idea of the religious-secular binary; the rise of science and the spread of new technologies all contributed to the transformation of prevailing paradigms of justice.[25] But of all these changes, colonialism raised the greatest questions of political power, sovereignty and the route to achieve agency, and consequently shaped emerging discourses on justice.

In the center of this process lies an important debate about the nature of the destabilization that colonialism wrought on the interrelationship between the legal, social and political domains of society. Wael Hallaq, in his provocative intervention *The Impossible State*, posits an inherent conflict between the ethical world of the Shariʿah and the western model of the state. The nature of this conflict resides in the way in which the law operated within a premodern Muslim social context compared to the modern western state. Hallaq argues that the law in the premodern Shariʿah "[was] a primarily social, and not a political, phenomenon. It is identified with society, and not the 'state,' regardless of how the 'state' is defined."[26] Drawing on the German legal and political theorist Carl Schmitt, who provides one of the most influential conceptual definitions of the western state,[27] Hallaq contends that colonialism led to the state encompassing the social, cultural and economic domains of society, which posed a problem for Muslims at an ontological level. He thus characterizes the modern state as "impossible", because it forecloses the space for the ethical and moral realization of the Muslim citizen.[28]

But while Hallaq argues in a philosophical register that the modern state cannot be refashioned to accommodate appeals to moral agency for Muslims, colonial-era Muslim intellectuals did in practice contend with the nation state in various political ways. This included advocating for more just social and political relations in Muslim majority nations, calling for the establishment of new, "Islamic" states and problematizing the concept of the modern nation state. In fact, the period of colonialism witnessed a change in the authority of Islamic scholars, bringing Islamic intellectuals into the forefront of debates and political movements centered on justice in society. The ulema steadily lost authority both due to the fragmentation and power vacuums opened by colonial rule and due to the technology of the printing press and the collapse of social barriers to knowledge, which resulted in foundational texts gaining a wider popular distribution throughout society.[29] Religious intellectual activity was no longer limited to the ulema, but now included figures who had gained a popular political or social appeal. Modern reformers of Islamic thought were trained in western academic settings as well as traditional Islamic centers of learning and they frequently participated directly in major political movements, uprisings and revolutions while contributing to the key debates of their time.

In the context of colonialism, the intellectual task tended to revolve around the question of the state as a barrier to the achievement of justice.[30] Justice was thus no longer immanent to the existing social relations, but became a future-oriented concept due to the oppressive nature of colonial society. Thought in tandem with a more total reinvention or destruction of the state, justice became a deeply political concept to be realized only after a far-reaching social revolution. The ideas of Sayyid Quṭb, the highly influential Egyptian thought leader executed in 1966 and Abul A'la Mawdudi, the Indian political and theological thinker who died in 1979, stand out as exemplary in this regard. For these intellectuals, known widely as pioneers of "Islamism", justice was premised on a total overhaul of Islam's political place in the world.

In the case of Mawdudi, justice was understood within the context of the utopian political vision of a future Islamic state modeled on the rightly guided city of the Prophet, Madinah. As Roy Jackson, Irfan

Ahmad and others argue, Mawdudi's "theo-democracy" was formed in an agonistic dialogue with an array of western discourses on justice and equality, from Marxism, liberalism, and secularism, to communism.[31] These discourses posed as a discursive backdrop to his attempts to develop Islamic thinking on the political and put forward Islam as its own "ism." Yet despite his insistence on establishing a unique form of the Islamic state and his reluctance to admit such influences, Mawdudi's thinking must be understood in the light of modern western philosophical concerns.

Mawdudi's concept of the caliphate as a "transhistorical" phenomenon, for example, was arguably influenced by the prominent French philosopher Henri Bergson (d. 1941). Mawdudi's idea was that the perfect state of Madinah was not something that could be replicated in actual form but that it presented a transhistorical set of universal and absolute principles, a "spirit", that must serve as the ideal model for his own age.[32] In this regard, he seems to be drawing on Bergson's concept of the *élan vital* via its reception in the thought of the early twentieth-century Indian philosopher and poet, Muhammad Iqbal.[33]

The approach to justice adopted by Iqbal is markedly different from the Islamist impulse that sought a distinct epistemological ground for Muslim political thought. In his major work, *The Reconstruction of Religious Thought in Islam*, he presents a cosmopolitan vision that calls for epistemic collaboration between European and Islamic philosophical insights based on the premise that European culture contains a deep symmetry with that of Islam.[34] Iqbal argued that the state must be thought of as a future-oriented Islamic entity, not tethered to the pristine ideals of the past. While Iqbal's political vision would shape the contours of modern Pakistan, his influence on Muslim ethical thought in the postcolonial period up to the present was less influential given his insistence on connecting Islam to western modes of thinking. The rise of Salafi thought during the early twentieth century challenged his future-oriented conception of the caliphate. For Iqbal, one of the hallmarks of Islamic political philosophy was the way it treated time as a continuous flow, making the idea of an Islamic state tethered to the past an anathema.[35]

Another movement with origins in the colonial era that promoted justice is the Muslim Brotherhood, founded in 1928 by Ḥasan al-Banna, an Egyptian political activist and intellectual. A basic principle of the Muslim Brotherhood was that westernization posed a danger to Muslim societies.

Unlike Iqbal, who explicitly sought the invention of an Islamically inspired state, the challenge al-Banna and his followers faced was how to address present structural inequities of poverty and corruption in Egyptian society. Intellectually, this meant responding on a different footing to the ulema who had exhibited complicity with the corrupt state. Perhaps the best articulation of the Muslim Brotherhood's concept of justice is found in Sayyid Quṭb's *Social Justice in Islam* (*al-ʿAdālah al-ijtimāʿiyyah fī al-islām*).

For Quṭb, justice must be sought through the realization of the holistic values of Islam in society. Importantly, Quṭb expanded his conception of justice in dialogue with Marxist analyses that limited justice to the economic base of society, opting instead for a more universal justice that grounded all aspects of life on faith in God. While arguing that only the "absolute" justice of Islam provided an adequate answer to the problems plaguing Egyptian society and by extension the Muslim world, Quṭb did not propose that the state should be the primary arbiter of justice. Instead he advocated a more decentralized model of *shūrā* (consultation) as the proper means.[36] Through his attraction to the thought and political activism of Ḥasan al-Banna, Quṭb would be drawn to the Muslim Brotherhood, finding in its mission a more equitable form of justice that sought holistic solutions to social problems. The Muslim Brotherhood has remained an important locus for Muslim political thinking and activism up to the present, with the Qatar-based Egyptian jurist Yusuf al-Qaradawi the most prominent intellectual figure associated with the movement.

A profoundly significant political event of the late-twentieth century was the Iranian revolution of 1979, which signals the first time in the modern period that a religious body seized state power.[37] The intellectual figurehead of the Iranian revolution, Ayatollah Khomeini, held a similar vision of the role of the Shariʿah as a total force for the promotion of virtue in society to that of Mawdudi and Quṭb, and had the writings of these thinkers translated into Persian.[38] However, Khomeini favored a centralized, Islamically directed government as the primary implementing force for the Shariʿah.[39] His vision of justice was also combined with a strong critique of the corruption that westernization and the legacy of colonialism played in Iranian society. This message appealed to wide segments of the Iranian people, particularly the impoverished.

Postcoloniality: New Movements

In the latter part of the twentieth century up to the present there have been a number of diverse trends in contemporary justice movements and schools of political thought within the global Muslim community. Beginning in the postwar period, Islamism shifted its political discourse from an emphasis on seizing state power to a focus on the promotion of societal and political reform.[40] Justice became centered on the promotion of public morality and a more horizontal, grassroots expansion of Islam among the masses was emphasized.[41]

The postcolonial turn in Islamic political thought must be understood against the background of the transition of the global economy to a period of financial capitalism and the end of the bipolar power balance between American capitalism and USSR communism. In the post-Cold War world, majority Muslim societies experienced significant population booms that, combined with the forces of globalization, brought about a new segment of the middle class as well as growing lower classes. As access to Islamic education became widely accessible across Muslim majority societies, movements that emphasized the epistemic autonomy of Islamic thought from western modes of thinking became more prominent. For example, a significant trend emerging in the last two decades of the twentieth century was known as the Islamization of knowledge.

The idea that underlay the Islamization of knowledge movement was that there should not be a division of knowledge between secular and Islamic spheres, but that values drawn from the Islamic tradition could be used to reframe modern knowledge in an ethical direction. The realization of justice was thus a central theme. In 1978, the Malaysian scholar Syed Muhammad Naquib al-Attas wrote of '[t]he 'islamization' of present-day knowledge' in his book *Islām and Secularism*.[42] A parallel development occurred in the thought of the Palestinian-American scholar Isma'il Raji al-Faruqi, one of the founding figures of the International Institute of Islamic Thought (IIIT) in Pennsylvania in 1981. He presented his influential paper 'Islamization of Knowledge: Problems, Principles, and Prospective' at an international conference organized by IIIT and held in Islamabad, Pakistan, in 1982.[43] Al-Attas founded the International Institute of Islamic Thought and Civilization (ISTAC), based in Kuala Lumpur, in 1987.[44]

Recently scholars working under the auspices of IIIT have revisited and extensively critiqued the Islamization of knowledge paradigm with the conclusion that it failed to fully take account of embedded structural challenges to reform: 'there is a lack of awareness about how knowledge is produced in contemporary society, how disciplines have evolved and the functions they perform, and about the relationship between knowledge and worldview.'[45] This has resulted in IIIT reframing its work towards educational development in Muslim societies, hoping to realize its ethical goals through applied research and strategic dissemination. Though such pragmatic concerns about the social barriers inhibiting reform are valid, the epistemic question of whether there can be a decolonized form of Islamic knowledge able to articulate contemporary justice remains pressing and is relevant to several chapters of the present volume.

Related to Islamization of knowledge but focused more specifically on the reform of Islamic law is a general tendency that can be termed the *maqāṣid* movement. The term *maqāṣid al-sharīᶜah* refers to the so-called higher objectives of the Law and can be linked back to a classical discourse most prominently supported by Ashᶜarite theologians and jurists, such as Abū Maᶜālī al-Juwaynī (d. 478/1085), al-Ghazālī, Fakhr al-Dīn al-Rāzī (d. 606/1209), and influentially developed by al-Shāṭibī (d. 790/1388) in his text *Al-Muwāfaqāt fī uṣūl al-sharīᶜah*.[46] The classical idea was that certain general values, especially five necessities (*ḍarūriyyāt*), could be derived inductively from the revealed sources and then used to regulate the application of the law to ensure greater *maṣlaḥah* (public benefit), particularly in cases where the sources were silent.[47] During the last one hundred years, some Muslim thinkers have seen the *maqāṣid* as a fruitful theoretical approach to make sure that the justice of the Shariᶜah can be realized within the conditions of modernity. Figures such as Rashid Rida, Al-Ṭāhir Ibn ᶜAshūr, Muhammad al-Ghazali, Yusuf al-Qaradawi and Taha Jabir al-Alwani have all suggested adjustment to the necessities upheld within the classical *maqāṣid* theory, strongly emphasizing social justice themes.[48] But Anver Emon points out the irony that, despite the reformist aspirations of such jurists, the theory of *maqāṣid* was in fact historically developed in order to limit the kind of rational deliberation to which they call.[49] This is because, at least as classically understood, the *maqāṣid* are ontologically grounded on revelation and must remain within the bounds of the explicit textual rules of the sources.[50] Nevertheless, there are various trends within the modern *maqāṣid* movement, with some figures advocating groundedness in the source texts, while others use the historical pedigree of this jurisprudential discourse for reform objectives based on alternative ethical grounds.

The *maqāsid* in this latter sense can be considered a subset of an "ethical turn" in recent Muslim thought, which embraces a range of theoretical perspectives. Figures such as the Moroccan philosopher Taha Abderrahmane seek a radical reimagining of al-Shāṭibī's *maqāṣid al-sharīʿah* theory in terms of moral discourse. According to Ebrahim Moosa, the project of Abderrahmane "urges for a closer theoretical and practical relationship between law and morality while simultaneously correcting some aspects of the traditional framework in order to make it more robust."[51] Moreover, Abderrahmane's work on the *maqāṣid* is only a small part of his ethical project.[52] A second prominent thinker who seeks to radically revise *maqāṣid* discourse for ethical ends is the Swiss theologian Tariq Ramadan.[53] He proposes a multidimensional reading of the purposes of Islamic law that considers the human inner being in terms of spiritual needs; individual being in terms of outward needs; and societies and groups as a whole.[54] Furthermore, he insists that ethical values, such as justice, can only be achieved when theory allows textual analysis to enter into rich conversation with the applied knowledge of specialists working in contemporary scientific disciplines.[55]

Perhaps the most significant Muslim ethical thinker of the latter part of the twentieth century was the Pakistani intellectual Fazlur Rahman, who died in 1988. He focused on reconstructing the contextual background of the Qur'an in order to derive extrahistorical values, and above all justice, to be realised anew in the contemporary world.[56] This is a distinctive direction that puts questions of hermeneutics and history centre stage in Muslim ethical thinking. Though he neither provided a definitive methodology to search for moral values within scripture, nor to realize his proposed second stage of their application to the modern world, his approach has had a considerable impact on scholars amenable to reformism.[57] Fazlur Rahman was forced to flee Pakistan due to controversy over his theology of revelation, but then through his works authored at the University of Chicago has influenceed other non-Arab Muslim majority contexts such as Turkey and Indonesia.[58] He has also been an important figure in the development of new approaches to ethics within Western English-speaking academic contexts, with the Australian academic Abdullah Saeed a notable promoter of his "contextualist" approach.[59]

Another prominent theme in recent Muslim scholarship, both within Western academia and more broadly on the global stage, is a focus on gender justice. This intellectual movement, spearheaded by female Muslims seeking to reclaim the message of scriptural sources from what is seen as the injustice of their patriarchal context or traditional interpretation, draws from recent Muslim ethical thought as well as Western feminist theory. Some Muslim feminists (though not all authors accept the label)[60] focus their hermeneutics on the Qur'an and downplay the Hadith corpus due to the criticism it has received in twentieth-century Western academia and the additional challenge it represents to many contemporary ideas of gender justice. Moreover, figures such as amina wadud, Asma Barlas, and Jerusha Tanner Lamptey bypass the classical legal and exegetical disciplines in looking to rediscover the ethical core of scripture.[61] Other scholars have gone beyond the Qur'an, often analyzing the way in which various disciplines shape and restrict the range of potential meanings within normative religious texts and construct interpretative authority for the ulema. Notable contributions include the work of Fatima Mernissi, Kecia Ali, Ayesha Chaudhry and Karen Bauer, who, though not a Muslim, shares many scholarly sympathies with the approach.

In recent years, a number of these mainly US-based scholars have engaged in lively internal discussion and critique about the objectives, methods, successes, and failures of their ongoing project. The 2014 publication of Aysha Hidayatullah's *Feminist Edges of the Qur'an* offered a wide-ranging critique of the interpretative gymnastics arguably required to read the Qur'an in accordance with modern norms of gender justice.[62] Her research has led her to propose a potentially more radical theological program to undergird future ethical deliberation.[63] This accords with the recent direction of Lamptey in her book *Divine Words, Female Voices: Muslima Explorations in Comparative Feminist Theology*.[64] A response by wadud is to highlight the extent to which she sees her own legacy in terms of activism and praxis as much as theoretical scholarship,[65] a point that applies to the various subfields that study justice.

Postcolonial and decolonial articulations of justice have also emerged within academic spaces as important fields for thinking through discourses of power – hermeneutical, epistemological, institutional and political – that shape the lives of Muslims. In their critique of power, these fields of study offer a set of strategies for rethinking the place of universality in contemporary conversations around justice. For example, in the work of Salman Sayyid, founder of Critical Muslim Studies, the category of the universal is considered to exist in a state of crisis in the contemporary period. This crisis stems from the collapse of legitimacy for European and western liberal claims to universality in the arenas of justice, ethics and politics. But this opens new spaces in which Islamic claims to universality become more politically charged. Decolonial thought also discusses the role of identity in the construction of Muslim political agency and how multiculturalism and Eurocentrism present unique challenges to the identity formation of Muslims in the contemporary period.

The Future: Emerging Vistas

Scholarship on justice in Islam is rapidly developing. As evidenced by the contributions to this volume, the conversation is a global one, taking place inside and outside of academic departments and involving an engagement between Muslim thought drawn from diverse Islamic traditions and discourses from varied intellectual sources and histories. Though the chapters presented here offer just a snapshot, they gather modern thinkers based in countries including Japan, Morocco, the USA, Iran, and Turkey. It has become evident that within the scholarship of today, rootedness in a set of beliefs and practices does not negate the claim to universality, rather, as seen in light of the work of figures such as Taha Abderrahmane and Alasdair MacIntyre, it merely negates the assumed universality of the post-enlightenment West.[66] The discussions that can be held in this brave new world of scholarship are extremely rich, though there is an increased danger of speaking past one another due to incommensurable standards.

The shift away from many of the presuppositions of the theoretical and methodological edifice often termed orientalism, has led to the development of constructive theological positions by Muslims and in dialogue with them. Aaron Hughes, in his book *Islam and the Tyranny of Authenticity*, has argued that the arrival of theological discourse within the study of religion has resulted in apologetics disguised as critical scholarship.[67] But an alternative way to read the tea leaves is that strict boundaries between theology and critical religious studies, whether historical or otherwise, are themselves an ideological formation. In any field of scholarship, a scholar's perspective is fundamentally shaped by pre-existing commitments and the structure of their life world. It is better to persist with an awareness that commitments and perspectives are woven into scholarly activity and that such commitments do not lessen the quality or novelty of scholarship, than to assume that a metric of absolute critical objectivity is possible, let alone desirable.

Going forward, there is little value in categorizing the debate over justice as a contest between monoliths of Islam and the West, however these are to be constructed. Rather, there should be multidimensional discussions between the competing tendencies within each. In Islam, the threads of justice from earlier centuries may persist, albeit frayed, alongside their younger rivals. There is thus a need to critically deploy concepts from the Islamic tradition within new disciplinary contexts in response to modern problems. Within Islamic approaches to Western thought, though engagement with liberalism remains significant, other possibilities including new strands of Marxist, feminist and critical race theory demand careful attention in the context of justice. Moreover, changes in technology and society have provoked new questions relating to the environment and the nature of the human being that remain underdeveloped within contemporary Muslim thought, despite some promising initiatives in recent years.

The work showcased in this volume makes no claim to comprehensively address any of these thematic areas. But in drawing together five diverse chapters, it points towards some of the interesting theoretical paths that are emerging in global Muslim discussions of justice. The book is divided into two parts: Part 1: Theology, Ethics and Politics, looks at underlying theological, ethical and political questions that are at stake within contemporary attempts to move forward the Muslim intellectual discourse around justice. Part 2: Regional Discourses of Feminism and Hermeneutics, has a dual focus. Two of the chapters pay attention to the question of gender justice and the ways in which contemporary Muslim female scholars have provided new interpretive techniques and readings of Muslim scripture, history and law. All three chapters discuss how new directions for ideas of justice in Islam are embedded in scholarship emerging from regional contexts: Turkey, Iran, and Japan.

PART 1: Theology, Ethics and Politics

Monir Birouk's chapter 'Taha Abderrahmane's Ethics of *Iḥsān*: A Lopsided

Conception of Justice and Citizenship' presents a nuanced critical reflection on the ideas of perhaps the most significant contemporary Arab philosopher as they relate to justice. A prolific writer, Abderrahmane's body of work is becoming increasingly prominent in Western academia, especially through recent studies of his thought by Wael Hallaq. Birouk locates Abderrahmane's discourse on justice within prevailing Western debates by discussing his critique of both Rawlsian liberalism and communitarianism, before comparing his oeuvre to his rivals in the firmament of contemporary Moroccan philosophy Mohammed Abed al-Jabri and Abdessalam Yassine. He ultimately argues that Abderrahmane's emphasis on personal spirituality and morality undermines his contribution to social and political thought, especially in the post-Arab Spring moment.

Ramon Harvey's chapter 'Whose Justice? When Māturīdī Meets MacIntyre' proposes that the metatheory of tradition-constituted enquiry developed by Alasdair MacIntyre can be used as a method for staging ethical debate about the nature of justice between Islamic and liberal worldviews. He draws from a wide selection of MacIntyre's publications to assess his approach to tradition and his claim to be able to provide a potential resolution to incommensurable ethical stances between different traditions. He also analyzes MacIntyre's characterization of liberal theories of justice and their underlying form of rationality. Then Harvey presents his own constructive interpretation of an Islamic tradition from which to theorize justice, a rereading of the theological position adopted by the Muslim theologian Abū Manṣūr al-Māturīdī (d. 333/944). He concludes by making a preliminary attempt to suggest how the resources afforded by Māturīdism could engage the liberal perspective on the question of justice.

PART 2: Regional Discourses of Feminism and Hermeneutics

Philip Dorroll opens with a chapter entitled 'The Hermeneutics of Justice: Hidayet Şefkatli Tuksal and the Artistry of the Qur'an' that focuses on one of the most prominent female theologians in Turkey. Drawing on her groundbreaking work of 2000, *Projections of Misogynistic Discourse in Islamic Tradition*, Dorroll gauges her interpretive framework and argues that she skilfully expresses how the Qur'anic text acts as a point of contact between the eternality of God and the contingency of the world. He goes on to show how Tuksal applies her hermeneutic theory to the Qur'anic verse 4:34, which has proved difficult to explain in the light of prevailing contemporary ideas of justice and equality. Comparing her work with recent Muslim feminists in the West, Dorroll asks probing questions about the challenges facing scholars who seek to reinterpret the Qur'an and assesses how far Tuksal's theological ideas are able to advance the discourse.

Samaneh Oladi's chapter explores the possibilities and limits of achieving gender justice within a Shiʿite Islamic framework in contemporary Iran. She highlights the various strands of Islamic jurisprudence (*fiqh*) utilised by scholars in an effort to interpret the provisions for women's legal status. While "traditional jurisprudence (*fiqh-e taqlīdī*)", continues to advocate orthodox principles and enjoys majority support from traditionalist ulema, it is challenged by "dynamic jurisprudence (*fiqh-e pouya*)", which attempts to revive Islamic legal dynamism. The chapter highlights how such jurisprudence affords alternative spaces where laws pertaining to women's rights and gender justice are challenged and renegotiated. Ultimately, she contends that this dynamic jurisprudence, spearheaded by reformist ulema, is bridging the gap between the legal establishment and greater gender justice in the Islamic Republic of Iran.

In the final chapter, Xiaofei Tu examines the emergence of Islamic studies in Japan, a country that is often considered at the periphery of the Muslim world and its academic conversation. He examines the life and work of the two most prominent Japanese scholars of Islam, Okawa Shumei and Toshihiko Izutsu. By contextualizing their work through analysis of Japan's own opening up to the rest of the world in the nineteenth and twentieth centuries, he traces an encounter that provoked intense questions of political justice. Tu provides an assessment of the motivations and methods of the two figures drawn primarily from sources inaccessible to prevailing English-language scholarship, delivering an insight into a distinctively Japanese perspective on Islamic studies. He then develops an argument that the main contribution of Shumei and Izutsu to the question of justice in Islam is in their highlighting of distinctive political and spiritual themes that reflect the Japanese experience.

Acknowledgements

This volume emerged from the Summer Institute for Scholars organized by the International Institute for Islamic Thought at Herndon, VA in July

26-29, 2017. With the exception of the chapter by Philip Dorroll who did not attend the Summer Institute and kindly contributed later, drafts of these papers were circulated in advance and each presentation received two formal responses before extensive wider discussion. This allowed for a genuine meeting of minds and a coherent shaping of our intellectual concerns. We would like to extend our heartfelt appreciation to all of the contributors as well as to the scholars who participated in the seminar but were not able to publish in this collection. We have benefited greatly from reading and reflecting upon the work of all the scholars involved in this project and thank them for their diligence in responding to our comments on their chapter drafts. We note that two contributions were removed from the volume after we had completed our editorial work and, though we accept the publisher's right to make this decision, we feel that it is a great loss to the collection. We also acknowledge the efforts of the staff at IIIT, in particular Dr. Hisham Altalib, IIIT President, for his generous welcome and encouragement; Dr. Ermin Sinanovic for organizing the program and entrusting us with the volume; Obay Altaleb and Rana Shehada for working with us throughout the production process; and Saulat Pervez for administrating the Summer Institute.

Endnotes

1. Blaise Pascal, *Thoughts*, trans. W. F. Trotter (New York: P. F. Collier and Son, 1910), p.105.
2. As elaborated in the text, this reading of *fuḍūl* may explain the origin of the phrase better than the common translation of "virtuous." See Abū Manṣūr al-Azharī, *Muʿjam tahdhīb al-lughah*, ed. Riyāḍ Zakī Qāsim, 4 vols (Beirut: Dār al-Maʿrifah, 2001), v.3, p.2801.
3. ʿAbd al-Malik ibn Hishām, *al-Sīrah al-nabawiyyah*, 4 vols (Cairo: Dār al-Fikr li al-Turāth, 2004), v.1, p.91. Ibn Isḥāq's text is only extant in the recension of Ibn Hishām (d. 218/833). For details about the relationship of the two texts, see L. I. Conrad, 'Ibn Hishām (d. 218/833)', in *Encyclopedia of Arabic Literature, Volume 1*, eds. Julie Scott Meisami, Paul Starkey (London and New York: Routledge, 1998), p.335.
4. See Ramon Harvey, *The Qur'an and the Just Society* (Edinburgh: Edinburgh University Press, 2018), pp.14-15.
5. For more discussion on the place of *nubuwwah* (prophecy) in the context of the Qur'an's discourse on justice and its "moral narrative", see Harvey, *The Qur'an and the Just Society*, pp.15-23.
6. Translations from the Qur'an in this introductory chapter are based on M. A. S. Abdel Haleem, *The Qur'an: English Translation and Parallel Arabic Text* (Oxford: Oxford University Press, 2010).
7. Charles Taylor, *A Secular Age* (Cambridge, MA: The Belknap Press of Harvard University Press, 2007), pp.37-41.
8. Harvey, *The Qur'an and the Just Society*, pp.81-84.
9. Harvey, *The Qur'an and the Just Society*, pp.94-95.
10. Abū Ḥanīfah, *Al-ʿĀlim wa-l-mutaʿallim riwāyat Abī Muqātil ʿan Abī Ḥanīfah raḍiya Allāhu ʿanhuma wa-yalīhi risālat Abī Ḥanīfah ilā ʿUthmān al-Battī thumma al-fiqh al-absaṭ riwāyat Abī Muṭīʿ ʿan Abī Ḥanīfah raḥimahum Allāh*, ed. Muḥammad Zāhid al-Kawtharī (Cairo: Maṭbaʿat al-Anwār, 1949), p.38.
11. See Abū Ḥanīfah, *Al-ʿĀlim wa-l-mutaʿallim*, p.40. Cf. Qur'anic verses 3:104; 3:110; 3:114; 9:71; 9:112; 22:41; 31:17.
12. See Michael Cook, *Commanding Right and Forbidding Wrong in Islamic Thought* (Cambridge: Cambridge University Press, 2004). Cook begins the book by discussing a particular incident involving Abū Ḥanīfah on pp.3-10.
13. See George F. Hourani, *Reason and Tradition in Islamic Ethics* (Cambridge: Cambridge University Press, 1985), pp.101-106.
14. Najam Haider, *Shīʿī Islam: An Introduction* (Cambridge: Cambridge University Press, 2014), pp.25-29, 80-81.
15. Harvey, *The Qur'an and the Just Society*, pp.28-33; Ramon Harvey, *Transcendent God, Rational World: A Māturīdī Theology* (Edinburgh: Edinburgh University Press, 2021), p.162; Ulrich Rudolph, *Al-Māturīdī and the Development of Sunnī Theology in Samarqand*, trans. Rodrigo Adem (Leiden: Brill, 2015), p.299.
16. Abū Ḥāmid al-Ghazālī, *Iḥyā' ʿulūm al-dīn*, 16 vols (Cairo: Lajnat Nashr al-Thaqāfah al-Islāmiyyah, 1937–38), v.7, pp.1282-83. The word *aḥlam* would usually be translated as "most forbearing" and *aʿaff* as "most chaste", however the rendering in the main text fits within the semantic fields of the Arabic terms and seems to be what al-Ghazālī has in mind.

17. Al-ʿIrāqī (d. 806/1403-4), who wrote a commentary on the hadiths cited within the Iḥyā' that is usually printed with the text, cites a hadith reference for all four of them. See al-Ghazālī, Iḥyā' ʿulūm al-dīn, pp.1282-83.
18. Plato, *The Republic of Plato*, trans. Allan Bloom, 2nd edn (New York: HarperCollins, 1991), pp.105-14.
19. Ovamir Anjum, *Politics, Law, and Community in Islamic Thought: The Taymiyyan Moment* (Cambridge: Cambridge University Press, 2012), pp.173-77.
20 See Anjum, *Politics, Law, and Community in Islamic Thought*, pp.228-44.
21. Colin Imber, *Ebu's-su'ud: The Islamic Legal Tradition* (Edinburgh: Edinburgh University Press, 1997), pp.269-71.
22. Wael B. Hallaq, *The Impossible State: Islam, Politics, and Modernity's Moral Predicament* (New York: Columbia University Press, 2012), pp.68-69.
23. Abdulaziz Sachedina, *The Just Ruler in Shi'ite Islam: The Comprehensive Authority of the Jurist in Imamite Jurisprudence* (Oxford: Oxford University Press, 1988), pp.18-19.
24. Marcia Hermanson, 'Shah Walliullah (1703-62)' in T*he Princeton Encyclopedia of Islamic Political Thought, ed. Gerhard Bowering* (Princeton, NJ: Princeton University Press, 2013), pp.493-94.
25. Shahab Ahmed, *What is Islam?: The Importance of Being Islamic* (Princeton, NJ: Princeton University Press, 2016), pp.514-15.
26. Hallaq, *The Impossible State*, p.186.
27. Hallaq follows Schmitt in arguing that liberalism relegates the state to a God-like status and contends that this is ultimately incompatible with an Islamic concept of the state. See Carl Schmitt, *The Concept of the Political* (University of Chicago Press, 2007), p.32.
28. Hallaq, *The Impossible State*, pp.203-204.
29. Muhammad Qasim Zaman, 'The Ulama and Contestations on Religious Authority', in *Islam and Modernity*, eds. Muhammad Khalid Masud, Armando Salvatore and Martin van Bruinessen (Edinburgh: Edinburgh University Press, 2004), pp.206-36.
30. For example, the question of the proper role of the state played a major role in intellectual debate within colonial independence movements in Pakistan, Algeria, Egypt and elsewhere.
31. Roy Jackson, *Mawdudi and Political Islam* (Abingdon: Taylor and Francis, 2004), pp.89-90; Irfan Ahmad, *Islamism and Democracy in India: The Transformation of Jamaat-e-Islami* (Princeton, NJ: Princeton University Press, 2009), pp.67-68.
32. Seyyed Vali Raza Nasr, *Mawdudi and the Making of Islamic Revivalism* (Oxford: Oxford University Press, 1996), p.51.
33. See Jackson, *Mawdudi and Political Islam*, pp.91-94.
34. Muhammad Iqbal, *The Reconstruction of Religious Thought in Islam* (Stanford, CA: Stanford University Press, 2013), p.6.
35. Iqbal, T*he Reconstruction of Religious Thought in Islam*, p.102.
36. Sayyid Quṭb, *al-ʿAdālah al-ijtimāʿiyyah fi al-islām* (Cairo: Dār al-Shurūq, 1995), pp.82-83.
37. Antony Black, *The History of Islamic Political Thought from the Prophet to the Present* (Edinburgh: Edinburgh University Press, 2001), p.319.
38. Black, *The History of Islamic Political Thought from the Prophet to the Present*, p.316.
39. Said Amir Arjomand, *The Shadow of God and the Hidden Imam: Religion, Political Order, and Societal Change in Shi'ite Iran from the Beginning to 1890* (Chicago, IL: University of Chicago Press, 1988), p.191.

40. Olivier Roy, *The Failure of Political Islam*, trans. Carol Volk (Cambridge: Harvard University Press, 1996), pp.100-101.
41. Roy, *The Failure of Political Islam*, p.76.
42. Syed Muhammad Naquib Al-Attas, *Islām and Secularism*, 2nd edn (Kuala Lumpur: International Institute of Islamic Thought and Civilization, 1993), p.162.
43. See Isma'il Raji al-Faruqi, 'Islamization of Knowledge: Problems, Principles and Prospective', in *Islam: Source and Purpose of Knowledge* (Herndon, VA: International Institute of Islamic Thought, 1988), pp.13-63.
44. Mona Abaza, *Debates on Islam and Knowledge in Malaysia and Egypt: Shifting Worlds* (London: Routledge, 2002), p.92.
45. Sardar, 'From Islamization to Integration of Knowledge', p.93.
46. Aḥmad al-Raysūnī, *Imām Al-Shāṭibī's Theory of the Higher Objectives and Intents of Islamic Law*, trans. Nancy Roberts (London: International Institute of Islamic Thought, 2005), pp.1-37.
47. See Harvey, *The Qur'an and the Just Society*, pp.39-40.
48. Jasser Auda, *Maqāṣid al-Sharīʿah as Philosophy of Islamic Law: A Systems Approach* (London: The International Institute of Islamic Thought, 2008), pp.6, 8.
49. Anver M. Emon, 'Sharia and the (Em)brace of Difference: From Theology to Law to Identity Politics', in *The Kuyper Center Review, Volume 2: Revelation and Common Grace*, ed. John Bowlin. Grand Rapids (MI: William B. Eerdmans Publishing Company, 2011), p.197.
50. Harvey, *The Qur'an and the Just Society*, p.40.
51. Ebrahim Moosa, 'On Reading Shāṭibī in Rabat and Tunis', in *Maqāṣid al-Sharīʿa and Contemporary Muslim Reformist Thought*, ed. Adis Duderija (New York: Palgrave Macmillan, 2014), p.187.
52. Ramon Harvey, 'Qur'anic Values and Modernity in Contemporary Islamic Ethics: Taha Abderrahmane and Fazlur Rahman in Conversation', in *Islamic Ethics and the Trusteeship Paradigm: Taha Abderrahmane's Philosophy in Comparative Perspectives*, ed. Mohammed Hashas and Mutaz al-Khatib (Leiden: Brill, 2020), pp.152-55.
53. We acknowledge the controversy surrounding Ramadan due to multiple rape allegations against him, as well as over the nature of his detention and treatment by the French authorities. At the time of writing, he has not been convicted of any of the rape allegations, though he has admitted to consensual extramarital affairs that are inconsistent with his Islamic principles.
54. Tariq Ramadan, *Radical Reform: Islamic Ethics and Liberation* (Oxford: Oxford University Press, 2009), pp.141-43.
55. Ramadan, *Radical Reform*, pp.130-33.
56. Fazlur Rahman, *Islam and Modernity: Transformation of an Intellectual Tradition* (Chicago: University of Chicago Press, 1982), pp.5-6.
57. See Harvey, 'Qur'anic Values and Modernity in Contemporary Islamic Ethics'.
58. Abdelwahab El-Affendi, 'The People on the Edge: Religious Reform and the Burden of the Western Muslim Intellectual', *Harvard Middle Eastern and Islamic Review* 8 (2009), pp.32-33; Felix Körner, *Revisionist Koran Hermeneutics in Contemporary Turkish University Theology: Rethinking Islam* (Würzburg: Ergon Verlag, 2005), p.109.
59. Abdullah Saeed, *Reading the Qur'an in the Twenty-First Century: A Contextualist Approach* (Abingdon: Routledge, 2014), p.23.

60. Aysha A. Hidayatullah, *Feminist Edges of the Qur'an* (Oxford: Oxford University Press, 2014), p.4.
61. amina wadud, *Qur'an and Woman: Rereading the Sacred Text from a Woman's Perspective* (Oxford: Oxford University Press, 1999), pp.1-3; Asma Barlas, "Believing Women" in *Islam: Unreading Patriarchal Interpretations of the Qur'an* (Austin, TX: University of Texas Press, 2002), pp.3-5; Jerusha Tanner Lamptey, *Never Wholly Other: A Muslima Theology of Religious Pluralism* (Oxford: Oxford University Press, 2014), pp.10-11.
62. Hidayatullah, *Feminist Edges of the Qur'an*, pp.150-51.
63. Aysha A. Hidayatullah, 'Claims to the Sacred', *Journal of Feminist Studies in Religion* 32(2) (2016), p.137.
64. Jerusha Tanner Lamptey, *Divine Words, Female Voices: Muslima Explorations in Comparative Feminist Theology* (Oxford: Oxford University Press, 2018), p.22.
65. amina wadud, 'Can One Critique Cancel all Previous Efforts?' *Journal of Feminist Studies in Religion* 32(2) (2016), p.131.
66. Mohammed Hashas, 'Taha Abderrahmane's Trusteeship Paradigm: Spiritual Modernity and the Islamic Contribution to the Formation of a Renewed Universal Civilization of Ethos', *Oriente Moderno* 95 (2015), pp.1-3.
67. Hughes, Aaron *Islam and the Tyranny of Authenticity: An Inquiry Into Disciplinary Apologetics* (Equinox Publishing Limited, 2015), p.22.

Bibliography

Abdel Haleem, M. A. S., *The Qur'an: English Translation and Parallel Arabic Text*. Oxford: Oxford University Press, 2010.

Abū Ḥanīfah, *Al-ʿĀlim wa-l-mutaʿallim riwāyat Abī Muqātil ʿan Abī Ḥanīfah raḍiya Allāhu ʿanhuma wa-yalīhi risālat Abī Ḥanīfah ilā ʿUthmān al-Battī thumma al-fiqh al-absaṭ riwāyat Abī Muṭīʿ ʿan Abī Ḥanīfah raḥimahum Allāh*, ed. Muḥammad Zāhid al-Kawtharī. Cairo: Maṭbaʿat al-Anwār, 1949.

Ahmed, Shahab, *What is Islam?: The Importance of Being Islamic. Princeton*, NJ: Princeton University Press, 2016.

Anjum, Ovamir, *Politics, Law, and Community in Islamic Thought: The Taymiyyan Moment*. Cambridge: Cambridge University Press, 2012.

Arjomand, Said Amir, *The Shadow of God and the Hidden Imam: Religion, Political Order, and Societal Change in Shi'ite Iran from the Beginning to 1890*. Chicago, IL: University of Chicago Press, 1988.

Auda, Jasser, *Maqāṣid al-Sharīʿah as Philosophy of Islamic Law: A Systems Approach*. London: The International Institute of Islamic Thought, 2008.

Barlas, Asma, "Believing Women" in *Islam: Unreading Patriarchal Interpretations of the Qur'an*. Austin, TX: University of Texas Press, 2002.

Black, Antony, *The History of Islamic Political Thought from the Prophet to the Present*. Edinburgh: Edinburgh University Press, 2001.

Conrad, L. I., 'Ibn Hishāṃ (d. 218/833)', in *Encyclopedia of Arabic Literature, Volume 1*, eds. Julie Scott Meisami, Paul Starkey. London and New York: Routledge, 1998.

Cook, Michael, *Commanding Right and Forbidding Wrong in Islamic Thought*. Cambridge: Cambridge University Press, 2004.

El-Affendi, Abdelwahab, 'The People on the Edge: Religious Reform and the Burden of the Western Muslim Intellectual', *Harvard Middle Eastern and Islamic Review*, 8 (2009), pp.19-50.

Emon, Anver M., 'Sharia and the (Em)brace of Difference: From Theology to Law to Identity Politics', in *The Kuyper Center Review, Volume 2: Revelation and Common Grace*, ed. John Bowlin. Grand Rapids, MI: William B. Eerdmans Publishing Company, 2011, pp.173-199.

al-Ghazālī, Abū Ḥāmid, *Iḥyā' ʿulūm al-dīn*. 16 vols. Cairo: Lajnat Nashr al-Thaqāfa al-Islāmiyya, 1937–38.

Haider, Najam, *Shīʿī Islam: An Introduction*. Cambridge: Cambridge University Press, 2014.

Hallaq, Wael B., *The Impossible State: Islam, Politics, and Modernity's Moral Predicament*. New York: Columbia University Press, 2012.

Harvey, Ramon, *The Qur'an and the Just Society*. Edinburgh: Edinburgh University Press, 2018.

——, 'Qur'anic Values and Modernity in Contemporary Islamic Ethics: Taha Abderrahmane and Fazlur Rahman in Conversation', in *Islamic Ethics and the Trusteeship Paradigm: Taha Abderrahmane's Philosophy in Comparative Perspectives*, ed. Mohammed Hashas and Mutaz al-Khatib. Leiden: Brill, 2020.

——, *Transcendent God, Rational World: A Māturīdī Theology*. Edinburgh: Edinburgh University Press, 2021.

Hermanson, Marcia, 'Shah Walliullah (1703-62)' in *The Princeton Encyclopedia of Islamic Political Thought*, ed. Gerhard Bowering. Princeton, NJ: Princeton University Press, 2013.

Hidayatullah, Aysha A., *Feminist Edges of the Qur'an*. Oxford: Oxford University Press, 2014.

——, 'Claims to the Sacred', *Journal of Feminist Studies in Religion* 32(2) (2016), pp.134-38.

Hourani, George F., *Reason and Tradition in Islamic Ethics*. Cambridge: Cambridge University Press, 1985.

Ibn Hishām, ʿAbd al-Malik. *al-Sīrat al-nabawiyya*. 4 vols. Cairo: Dār al-Fikr lil-Turāth, 2004.

Imber, Colin, *Ebu's-su'ud: The Islamic Legal Tradition*. Edinburgh: Edinburgh University Press, 1997.

Iqbal, Muhammad, *The Reconstruction of Religious Thought in Islam*. Stanford, CA: Stanford University Press, 2013.

Jackson, Roy, *Mawdudi and Political Islam*. Abingdon: Taylor and Francis, 2004.

Körner, Felix, *Revisionist Koran Hermeneutics in Contemporary Turkish University Theology: Rethinking Islam*. Würzburg: Ergon Verlag, 2005.

Lamptey, Jerusha Tanner, *Never Wholly Other: A Muslima Theology of Religious Pluralism*. Oxford: Oxford University Press, 2014.

___, *Divine Words, Female Voices: Muslima Explorations in Comparative Feminist Theology*. Oxford: Oxford University Press, 2018.

Moosa, Ebrahim, 'On Reading Shāṭibī in Rabat and Tunis', in *Maqāṣid al-Sharīʿa and Contemporary Muslim Reformist Thought*, ed. Adis Duderija. New York: Palgrave Macmillan, 2014, pp.177-192.

Pascal, Blaise, *Thoughts*, trans. W. F. Trotter. New York: P. F. Collier and Son, 1910.

Rahman, Fazlur, *Islam and Modernity: Transformation of an Intellectual Tradition*. Chicago: University of Chicago Press, 1982.

Ramadan, Tariq, *Radical Reform: Islamic Ethics and Liberation*. Oxford: Oxford University Press, 2009.

Al-Raysūnī, Aḥmad, *Imām Al-Shāṭibī's Theory of the Higher Objectives and Intents of Islamic Law*, trans. Nancy Roberts. London: International Institute of Islamic Thought, 2005.

Roy, Olivier, *The Failure of Political Islam*, trans. Carol Volk. Cambridge: Harvard University Press, 1996.

Rudolph, Ulrich, *Al-Māturīdī and the Development of Sunnī Theology in Samarqand*, trans. Rodrigo Adem (Leiden: Brill, 2015).

Saeed, Abdullah, *Reading the Qur'an in the Twenty-First Century: A Contextualist Approach*. Abingdon: Routledge, 2014.

Sardar, Ziauddin, 'From Islamization to Integration of Knowledge', in *Rethinking Reform in Higher Education: From Islamization to Integration of Knowledge*, ed. Ziauddin Sardar and Jeremy Henzell-Thomas. Herndon, VA: International Institute of Islamic Thought, 2017, pp.86-140.

Sachedina, Abdulaziz, *The Just Ruler in Shi'ite Islam: The Comprehensive Authority of the Jurist in Imamite Jurisprudence*. Oxford: Oxford University Press, 1988.

Taylor, Charles, *A Secular Age*. Cambridge, MA: The Belknap Press of Harvard University Press, 2007.

wadud, amina, *Qur'an and Woman: Rereading the Sacred Text from a Woman's Perspective*. Oxford: Oxford University Press, 1999.

___, 'Can One Critique Cancel all Previous Efforts?' *Journal of Feminist Studies in Religion* 32(2) (2016), pp.130-34.

Zaman, Muhammad Qasim, 'The Ulama and Contestations on Religious Authority' in *Islam and Modernity*, eds. Muhammad Khalid Masud, Armando Salvatore and Martin van Bruinessen. Edinburgh: Edinburgh University Press, 2009, pp.206-36.

PART 1

THEOLOGIES, ETHICS AND POLITICS

1

Taha Abderrahmane's Ethics of Iḥsān: A Lopsided Conception of Justice and Citizenship

Monir Birouk

Taha Abderrahmane is one of the most prominent philosophers of ethics in the Arab-Islamic world today. Leaning on the Islamic tradition, he constructs a spiritual and praxeological view of ethics that goes against the grain of the rational Enlightenment conception that most modernist Arab intellectuals embrace. By praxeological ethics in this context, I mean embodied and person-centered ethics – which are characteristic of religious ethics – as opposed to theoretical and abstract conceptions. One aspect of his moral philosophy that I think is especially relevant to Muslim societies in the years following the "Arab Spring" is his conception of citizenship and justice. In this chapter, I argue that Taha Abderrahmane's Islamic philosophical critique of secular ethics, both liberal and communitarian, is compromised by his account of ethics that underscores the spiritual experience and the moral duties of the individual at the expense of a thorough account of social and political justice.

To unpack this argument, I divide my chapter into three parts. In the first part, I outline Taha Abderrahmane's moral-cum-spiritual critique of liberal citizenship, particularly his critique of John Rawls's liberal theory of justice. In the second part, I stake out Taha Abderrahmane's engagement with communitarian thinkers with whom he converges on the critique of the liberal position, yet disagrees on the nature and boundaries of the community. In the last part, I argue that his conception of justice and citizenship is lopsided. In precise terms, I argue that Abderrahmane's conception of ethics, significant as it is especially in response to triumphalist secular ethics, is confined to a moralistic and spiritualistic discourse that ignores other conditions of social and political justice in Islam.

Critique of Liberal Justice: Justice as Devotion and Duty

Taha Abderrahmane engages with John Rawls's political theory of justice on two occasions: in his 2006 book *Rūḥ al-ḥadāthah: al-madkhal ilā ta'sīs al-ḥadāthah al-islāmiyyah* (*The Spirit of Modernity: Introduction to the Establishment of Islamic Modernity*) and briefly in his 2005 work *al-Ḥaqq al-islāmī fī al-ikhtilāf al-fikrī* (*The Islamic Right for Intellectual Difference*). He considers Rawls's conception of liberal citizenship as paradigmatic of the detachment of law and politics from morality in modern societies. Abderrahmane counters this materialist and rights-based conception of justice with a duty-based conception that is grounded in the ethics of *iḥsān*. This term designates the virtues of devotion, love, modesty, charity and excellence, particularly in contrast to the mode of religiosity that reduces Islam solely to a set of dry commands, obligations and prohibitions.

John Rawls is credited with the elaboration of the first substantive liberal conception of citizenship in his book *A Theory of Justice* in 1971. In this book as well as in his subsequent works, he translates his interpretation of Kantian deontological ethics into a political theory of justice that presupposes a constitutional democratic society. Since his theory of justice is liberal in character, it is evidently concerned with maximizing individual liberty and rights. For that matter, Rawls proposes a hypothetical framework where self-interested rational individuals agree behind the "veil of ignorance" on fair principles of justice. What he means by this is the position that is agreed upon by citizens who are veiled from their own interests. From this "original position" as Rawls calls it, equal and free citizens agree on a political conception of justice whereby "all social primary goods – liberty and opportunity, income and wealth, and the bases of self-respect – are to be distributed equally, unless an unequal distribution of any or all of these goods is to the advantage of the least favored."[1] Rawls's conception of liberal citizenship has, since the publication of his book, been widely adopted and adapted in political theory as well as in other fields. However, its basic assumptions have also been seriously contested and severely criticized, mainly by communitarian critics.[2]

Taha Abderrahmane's engagement with Rawls is both deconstructive and constructive. In this section I discuss the arguments that he advances to rebut Rawls's position. Abderrahmane highlights the contrived operations of separation that liberal thought – and by extension modernity – forces on human existence. To counter this tendency for separation and division, he proposes a holistic model of citizenship grounded in the moral and spiritual commitment of the individual and the community at large, and not in law or rights.

To begin with, Taha Abderrahmane locates the first instance of separation in Rawls's liberal citizenship in the idea of the original position. He discerns a shaky foundation for the principles of justice in this concept. The idea of the original position is a hypothetical representation, which Rawls proposes in order to set the condition for a fair agreement on the principles of justice between citizens who stand behind the veil of ignorance. Taha Abderrahmane contends that this idea is paradoxical. On the one hand, Rawls requires the individuals to "suppose in their minds" the conditions for a just citizenship, but requires them on the other to "actively engage in real political and social participation."[3] Rawls, therefore, creates a divide between the "illusionary foundation" of his liberal conception of citizenship and the "realistic demand of participation" of the citizens in social and political life in accordance with the principles that ensued from this agreement.[4] The philosopher Donald Dworkin makes a similar argument albeit from a different position. For him, what follows from an agreement between citizens in a hypothetical situation should also be hypothetical.[5]

As a substitute for Rawls's idea of the original position, Abderrahmane proposes the Islamic moral principle of sincere devotion (*ikhlās*). Disengagement from interests and egoistic drives can better be achieved through the actual moral of devotion than by the illusionary idea of the original position. In broad moral terms, he defines devotion as the constant and lifelong attempt of the individual to "disengage from all the causes that lead to injustice" through his connection with the Divine Being, the ultimate model of justice.[6] In return, God "reveals Himself through His just judgments" to the devout citizen who strives in the way of God to rid himself of the causes of injustice both towards himself through self-purification (*mujāhadah*) and towards others through struggle (*jihād*).[7] Taha Abderrahmane thus concludes that a citizenship founded on the ethics of devotion to God is, contrary to Rawls's hypothetical agreement, "real" and "constant."[8] Because the political and social participation of the citizen is founded on his constant devotion to divine justice, it is not only more solid, but also more certain and realistic than Rawls's hypothetical and shaky contractual agreement.

Taha Abderrahmane is certainly justified in his criticism of the unrealistic character of John Rawls's idea of the original position. In the Islamic worldview, the overarching principles of justice are set not by human beings, but by God who is the ultimate model of justice. Therefore, the best way to be detached from the interests and illegitimate aspirations of the self is through the connection with the Just. In other words, the veil between the human being and the Just has to be lifted and not drawn! Nevertheless, it seems to me that Abderrahmane misunderstood Rawls; the latter posits the original position only as a theoretical justification for justice, which is indeed common to all social contract theories. As such, Rawls does not claim that people should base their adherence to the liberal conception of justice on it as Abderrahmane understands. After all, by the same logic, a person who does not share Taha Abderrahmane's Islamic worldview could adduce the primordial Covenant of Alast, which Abderrahmane emphasizes, as a rebuttal to his argument.[9] This is because the Covenant of Alast occupies in Abderrahmane's philosophy the same role as the original position in Rawls's theory of justice. His theorization of the trusteeship of the human being (*i'timāniyyat al-insān*) – by which he means the original human state of spiritual and moral responsibility – is ultimately predicated on the Covenant of Alast. The point I am making here is that unless one positions himself or herself within the Islamic sphere, Abderrahmane's counterargument that the idea of original position is hypothetical is not compelling. Rawls presupposes a liberal conception of society in the same way that the idea of the Convention of Alast presupposes adherence to the Islamic worldview.

In addition, Taha Abderrahmane also misses the true idea that the original position aims to emphasize. The idea of the citizens who stand behind the veil of ignorance is a heuristic device or thought experiment, which is meant to emphasize two notions that are presupposed by any fair agreement about justice: equality and freedom. For Rawls, it is only by being veiled from any knowledge about their natural endowments, their future as well as their conception of the good life, that citizens can be equal and free.[10] These two conditions of freedom and equality are the locus of Rawls's endeavor. Unfortunately, Taha Abderrahmane is too preoccupied with the illusionary character of the original position in Rawls's theory to recognize the significance of these two values.

In contemporary political philosophy, striking the balance between liberty and equality is a challenge that any theory of justice has to address.[11] From an Islamic perspective, it would be, for instance, worthwhile to explain how the concepts of equality and freedom are central to the ethical scheme, how they are often undermined or compromised – sometimes in the name of religion itself – and how they could be accommodated with and applied in modernized societies.[12] Disappointingly, Taha Abderrahmane divorces, though unintentionally I think, the moral discourse from political and institutional realities.

The second objection Taha Abderrahmane has to Rawls's theory of justice concerns its individualistic character. For him, Rawls's liberal citizen is an "individuated self", which is detached from its community.[13] In Rawls's liberal scheme, Taha Abderrahmane argues, what the citizens are concerned about before and after their contractual agreement is "getting rights that are equal to those of other citizens as well as broadening the sphere of these rights as much as possible."[14] In this materialist-based conception of justice, public interest and the care for the other are hardly the concern of the liberal citizen.

Abderrahmane shares this concern over the egoism and self-centeredness of the liberal citizen with the communitarian philosophers who are disconcerted by Rawls's oblivion of the role of the community in the constitution of the individual. In *Liberalism and the Limits of Justice*, the communitarian philosopher Michael Sandel argues that the "assumption of mutual disinterest introduces an individualistic bias which rules out or...devalue[s] such motives as benevolence, altruism and communitarian sentiments."[15] Alasdair MacIntyre and Charles Taylor, also often considered communitarians, articulate the same concern about the individualistic character of Rawls's theory.[16]

For both Taha Abderrahmane and the communitarians, the role of the community, and by extension tradition, is crucial to the constitution of the individual. The individual is ingrained in his community, and he is necessarily, either positively or negatively, shaped by it. Abderrahmane introduces the ethics of devotion as a substitute to the disinterested and law-centered character of the liberal citizen. By virtue of his constant devotion to God – one of whose ninety-nine names is the Just – the citizen does not relate to other citizens in a legalistic and rights-based manner as Rawls seems to suggest. Instead, he is morally required, in addition to abiding by the precepts of justice, to "give precedence to duties over rights" and not vice versa.[17] More than that, justice that is grounded in religious ethics supports several modalities of ethical conduct. Thus, the relationship of the devout citizen to others can take different modes that range from "fairness...to charity...and...love."[18] These theologically based virtues construct a moral space where the intersubjective relation of the citizen to other citizens constitutes a powerful antidote to the cold and iron-caged individualism of liberalism, and of secular ethics at large.

The third objection Taha Abderrahmane adduces against the separation between law and ethics in Rawls's conception of liberal citizenship concerns the nature of the human self. For Rawls, the citizen in the original position is veiled not only from his natural endowments, but also from his "conception of the good" lest the latter would negatively affect his view of justice. In the liberal society – and after the veil is lifted – the citizen should also draw a clear-cut line between his conception of the good, which Abderrahmane translates as "the moral view", and the public good. The wisdom behind this separation is that the citizens who embrace different and often irreconcilable notions of justice cannot come to agree on a single one in the public sphere if they do not agree to hold their beliefs, or conceptions of the good in Rawls's words, at bay.

From the perspective of the implicit religious position of the communitarians and the explicit religious position of Taha Abderrahmane, Rawls presupposes an unseemly metaphysical notion of the self. For Abderrahmane, the Rawlsian notion of the citizen is incoherent as it presupposes a self that is divorced from any conception of the good. Rawls, he says, conceives of "two disparate selves", a "non-moral self" prior to the contractual agreement and a "moralized self" after the agreement.[19] For Sandel, this moral split of the subject is a natural consequence of Rawls's neo-Kantian "metaphysical deontology." This view, he argues, presupposes an "antecedently individuated subject" who is distanced from, and even exists prior to his ends.[20] In the same vein, Alasdair MacIntyre insists that the notion of the self presupposes a "narrative unity", and separating the self from its ends, or *telos* in the language of Aristotle, leaves us with an "emotivist self" that loses the objective criteria for making moral decisions.[21] For Taha Abderrahmane, this notion of a self that is detached from its moral ends is neither coherent nor desirable. Such *telos* can be achieved in the orientation of the individual towards his Creator and in his constant inner striving to rid himself of the causes of injustice.

In this respect, Taha Abderrahmane introduces an intriguing understanding of injustice. The latter, he argues, should be understood not only as the wrong, which the self incurs on another self, but also as the wrong the individual incurs on himself.[22] Doing injustice to oneself is a Qur'anic concept that puts emphasis on the self before interpersonal and institutional relationships.[23] A similar exploration of the relation of justice and injustice to the internal worlds of the self is found in the writings of Syed Muhammad Naquib Al-Attas. In his books *Islam: The Concept of Religion and the Foundation of Ethics and Morality* (1992) and *On Justice and the Nature of Man* (2015), Al-Attas argues that at the root of the injustice an individual incurs on his brothers and sisters in humanity is the wrong that he brings upon himself in the first place. In this sense, injustice can be done to the self not only by the well-off (who are unjust to others), but also by the wretched (who do not lead a virtuous life). In this case, the person adds the injustice that they bring upon themselves to the injustice to which they are subjected from without. More than that, "one can be unjust to oneself even as he believes that he exercises his right or that he is doing good to oneself."[24] Hence, all human beings, argues Abderrahmane, need to cultivate in themselves the "culture of pushing back self-injustice."[25] This framework is reminiscent of Michel Foucault's later turn towards what he calls the "technologies of the self" after his disenchantment with epistemology.

Abderrahmane's fourth and last argument contests Rawls's ubiquitous assertion of the priority of the right over the good. Rawls, and by extension all moral and political philosophers who embrace a secular worldview, not only separates the good and the right, but sets the latter as the ultimate standard for the definition of the former.[26] This view assumes that there can be a conception of the right that is neutral. But the concept of neutrality in the hard sciences, let alone in the realm of ethics, has long fallen from grace amongst philosophers. Echoing Alasdair MacIntyre in *Whose Justice? Which Rationality?*, Abderrahmane argues that there is no right that is not defined by the good. As he puts it: "justice itself is a good, and the principles and values that it underlies...such as equality, liberty, respect and tolerance also count as goods."[27] For both Taha Abderrahmane and the communitarians, the notion of neutrality, be it of rationality, of justice, or of the public sphere, is a myth.

This line of argument, of course, also problematizes the division between the public and the private spheres. From the perspective of Islamic ethics, these two realms are not envisaged as independent and separate. As Taha Abderrahmane puts it, morality "engulfs all actions" so that the good, which ultimately rests on belief, is always prior to the right.[28] In contrast to the inclination of modernity to separate the spheres of human activity, the fusion between religion – seen as a moral and theological force – and the law is congenial to Islamic legal and ethical theory.[29] In plain terms, law in the Islamic worldview depends on the moral worldview.

Critique of the Communitarians: The Ummah as a Global Moral Space

There is much on which the Islamic and communitarian conceptions of the self and ethics concur. However, Taha Abderrahmane does not spare them from his criticism either. To his mind, their insistence on the priority of the community and its ethics constitutes an extreme reaction to the individualism of liberal thought. The communitarians, he argues, affirm the role of the community in the constitution of the individual, and affirm the priority of the good over the right, but they eventually collapse ethics into the notion of the community. To counter this narrow conception of ethics, Abderrahmane introduces the concept of the Ummah that, in his view, underlies a broad and open understanding of moral values. Abderrahmane's venture against the communitarians is fraught with two major problems: he misrepresents the thought of the communitarians, and he dehistoricizes the idea of the Ummah.

For Taha Abderrahmane, the communitarians stance on citizenship is problematic, as their notion of the community leads them to a narrow understanding of it. While liberal citizenship does not allow for a morality that cares about social and communitarian bonds, the communitarian approach is too "secluded" and community-centered to allow for a "humanitarian ethics."[30] I find this judgment of Abderrahmane to be an overstatement based on a misreading of the communitarian literature. As I argue below, not all communitarians collapse ethics into community ethics, and it does not follow that community ethics is necessarily secluded and self-enclosed. Nevertheless, I endorse Abderrahmane's view that Islamic ethics is much more open to, and inclusive of, different communities and cultures.

Abderrahmane pinpoints three manifestations of this claimed seclusion. To begin with, the (over)valuation of the community and its past often drives the citizens to blindly cling to its history and values. This "blind loyalty", he says, might take the form of "reviving monuments and symbols" from the past or the "invention of mythical or syncretic tradition or history."[31] Second, communitarian citizens are more likely to emphasize the differences between their own community and other communities instead of working towards common and shared values. In this way, the community becomes more like "the social institution that organizes the seclusion of its members, and defends their specific cultural rights without providing them with the ways through which they would transcend such seclusion and come into relations with others."[32] The third manifestation of the narrowness of the communitarian conception of citizenship is its narrow understanding and practice of ethics. Communitarian ethics largely draws on the "inherited habits" and established modes of conduct by the community.

The community, thus conceived, harbors a conception of citizenship that is not only introverted and self-reflexive, but also materialistic. Its narrowness, Abderrahmane thinks, is manifested in the blind loyalty of the citizen to their own community; in the confinement of the citizen in the cultural specificity of the community; and in its stagnant ethics that is largely constituted by inherited habits. But the cause for this seclusion, he contends, is its materialistic character. Despite its valuation of morality and collective bonds, the communitarian conception of citizenship is, like its liberal counterpart, still partly materialistic in its aims. The motivation of the community is to a great extent to preserve its history and to ensure more cultural rights in a context of struggle against other communities. Although the communitarian conception of citizenship "incorporates both the private and the public spheres, and does not drive out the moral constituent from...the public sphere, it does not elevate [ethics] to an extent where [the public sphere] can harbor the highest spiritual values."[33] In other words, communitarian ethics as Abderrahmane understands it is too grounded in the history of the community to allow for a spiritual ethics that is open to the horizon of humanity.

In evaluating Taha Abderrahmane's critique of these community-centred ideas of justice, it is apparent that the positions he criticizes cannot always be identified with the communitarian conception of citizenship. One wonders whether his misrepresentation of the communitarians' ideas can be ascribed to a misunderstanding of their theses or, more alarmingly, to the desire to win the argument against a straw man.[34] Indeed, Taha Abderrahmane issues generalized statements about the communitarian conception of citizenship in his book *Rūḥ al-ḥadāthah* without engaging with any of their works. It would be more convincing, for example, if Abderrahmane developed his argument about the seclusion of communitarian ethics in light of the later MacIntyre's Thomistic position or Taylor's theorization of the "politics of recognition".

Taken out of context, some communitarian conceptions of the community might be interpreted along the lines of Taha Abderrahmane's criticism. To face the "dark ages" of the modern capitalistic moral chaos, Alasdair MacIntyre, for example, calls for the "construction of local forms of community within which civility and the intellectual and moral life can be sustained."[35] For that matter, MacIntyre's critique of liberal modernity is often criticized as a nostalgic desire that succumbs to the seduction of the past.[36] Taha Abderrahmane's criticism of the "seclusion" and "ossified ethics" of the communitarian conception of citizenship might also be justified when one deals with certain radical ideological and political articulations of communitarian thought. Once it is entrusted to the ideologues, the politicians and the activists, the community might cease to be a source of moral flourishing for individuals and become an idol to be reified, and an impediment to inter-communitarian dialogue, tolerance and mercy. But judging from the works of the communitarian thinkers to whom Abderrahmane refers, this worry is, more often than not, unwarranted.

Taha Abderrahmane refers to the Islamic concept of the Ummah that he theorizes as steering a middle course between the legalism of liberalism and the self-inclusion of the communitarian view. As such, it allows for the promotion of citizenship from mere coexistence to fraternity. In the moral space of the Ummah, the recognition of the different other and the openness to their culture are morally and spiritually motivated by the Islamic theological view. Abderrahmane pinpoints two characteristics that underpin the citizenship of fraternity in the Ummah: the realization of the moral essence of the human being and the capacity for the creative production of values.

To begin with, the Ummah is essentially a moral entity. In Taha Abderrahmane's words, it is a space where citizens strive to "internalize the moral essence" (*al-māhiyyah al-akhlāqiyyah*) that defines the nature of the human being.[37] Correspondingly, citizenship in the Ummah is predicated on two overarching conditions: utility in this world and benefit in the Hereafter. It is this otherworldly concern that distinguishes the Ummah from the communitarian conception of the community. It is true, the latter also grounds justice in a moral worldview, but its concerns are ultimately worldly; and any action that is confined to the world is marred by what Taha Abderrahmane calls "the political", à la Schmitt, which he equates with the will to domination (*tasayyud*). As I noted above, Abderrahmane's failure to deal with specific arguments of either Taylor, Sandel, MacIntyre or Walzer, compromises the accuracy of his judgment. One wonders for instance how his objection about the communitarians' "worldly" conception of the community applies to MacIntyre's and Taylor's Catholic ethics!

In addition to its essential moral view, the Ummah also provides its citizens with the capacity for the creative generation of values.[38] Unlike secular ethics, theistic ethics in general, and Islamic ethics in particular, incorporate different modalities of moral action. In contrast to modern moral philosophy, duty and utility are not mutually exclusive in Islamic ethics, and can both serve as motivations for the same moral action.[39] In this respect, theistic ethics and communitarian virtue ethics are deeply discontent with the bleak or "mercantile" – as Ross Poole put it – normative ethics of modernity, both in its deontological and utilitarian articulations.[40] However, the moral horizon that Abderrahmane ascribes to the Ummah also claims to transcend virtue ethics, particularly as it was articulated by MacIntyre before his later theistic turn. Here, Abderrahmane is probably more in line with the Canadian philosopher Charles Taylor. Both of them endorse an aesthetic view that envisages ethical rules not only as the objects of obedience or the pursuit of the good life, but primarily of love. In this view, the moral subject does not only ask, "what ought I to do?", as Kant exerts, or, "what good life should I pursue?" as the advocates of virtue ethics insist, but also, "what ought I to love?".[41] In the terminology of Taylor, morality is a constitutive good or "something the love of which empowers us to be and to do good."[42] In sum, the Ummah, unlike the community, does not cling to past habits and inherited ethics, but recreates its moral repertoire so that ethics is promoted from the status of mere "injunctions and prohibitions that subdue the will to the status of the aesthetic meanings that fill the souls, which are in turn transformed to epistemic ends that enlighten the reason."[43]

It is by dint of these two underpinnings, that is, the moral essence and the creative generation of moral values, that the Ummah comes to promote citizenship to the level of fraternity in a way that communitarian citizenship does not. The brotherly bond has its origin in the unity of the origin of human beings as creatures of God, and by this token it is more open and inclusive than national or community-based citizenship. To stake out this claim, Taha Abderrahmane draws on a moral language that has indiscreet Sufi overtones. In the Ummah, the citizen is enjoined to give priority to duties over rights and to treat others in accordance with *adab* or good manners. In *al-Ḥaqq al-islāmī fī al-ikhtilāf al-fikrī*, Abderrahmane pinpoints three morals that promote citizenship in the Ummah to the level of fraternity. The first of these is the moral of *al-hayā'* (an Islamic concept that combines both the senses of modesty and decency) whereby the community is "ashamed before God, before others and before itself to do something that is wrong and wicked."[44] The second moral is "moral struggle" (*al-jihād al-akhlāqī*), which is the constant "spiritual perseverance" to rid oneself of egoistic drives and to treat others in "accordance with the noblest of morals and virtues."[45] The third moral is "wisdom", and it is attained when reflection on the world of phenomena is founded on reflection on the world of signs – or "*vestigia dei*" in the Latin Biblical language. In other words, a rich and flourishing human existence should be connected with spiritual meaning and demarcated by ethical boundaries.

Abderrahmane's emphasis on the praxeological ethics of *iḥsān* undercuts two problematic understandings of the Ummah. First, he stresses the centrality of the moral and spiritual values against a nomocentric conception.[46] In the latter, the Qur'anic injunction to the Ummah to enjoin the good and to forbid the wrong is interpreted in a legalistic manner. In conjunction with this view, the Muslim community is represented as a body of believers who have to abide by divine commands, which are often conceived in a literalistic and de-contextualized way. The second misconception is of an ideological nature. The advocates of this view often cast the global Muslim community as a political entity whose existence is shaped by its adversarial position vis-à-vis cultural and civilizational others. It is to this sense that Olivier Roy refers when he speaks about the "supranational" ideological and political conceptions of the Ummah.[47] According to Abderrahmane, these distorted conceptualizations of the nature and function of the Ummah fall short of building a spirit of fraternity that transcends its boundaries.

A Lopsided Conception of Justice?

Taha Abderrahmane is a Muslim philosopher who has over the last four decades been competently engaged in the global battle of concepts. Unless Muslims fabricate their own concepts, he insists, they will remain under the intellectual tutelage of the dominant cultural other. From this perspective, his critical engagement with the liberal and communitarian conceptions of justice and citizenship flows into his endeavor to construct a theoretical paradigm of a morally grounded Islamic modernity.

Abderrahmane's deconstruction of secular ethics and defense of Islamic ethics is significant. His critique aims to deconstruct the epistemology of separation that undergirds the liberal conception of justice. The tendency of modernity to separate, which is inherited from Enlightenment thought, is manifested in the severance of ethics from religion, individual from community, the right from the good, and the public from the private. On the other hand, collapsing ethics into the moral view of the community in communitarian thought is also likely to enslave the citizen to the past values of their community. Stressing difference rather than consensus would ultimately shrink inter-communal bonds.

Taha Abderrahmane also demonstrates that the spiritual ethics of devotion, self-accountability, global fraternity, and the love of humanity offer a far better and more profound substitute for the impoverished conceptions of justice that are predicated on secular ethics. Such morals, with their accentuation of duties above rights, are undoubtedly much needed in an age where the reclamation of rights – and the gaining of additional rights – is the lingua franca of both individuals and communities.

Nevertheless, Abderrahmane's conceptualization of justice and citizenship remains lopsided. It is so because he provides us with a view that is both historically and politically detached. At the end of his analysis, we are left with an approach to justice that is grounded in spiritual ethics, but that ignores other conditions of possibility for establishing just citizenship. To be sure, our philosopher is right to stress the ethics of devotion, self-scrutiny and the observance of duties as the foundational conditions of citizenship and justice in a genuine Islamic community. These values have long been undermined by the juristic and political discourses that conceive of the Ummah either as a nomocentric community of believers, as an ideological entity, or both. But Taha Abderrahmane should also realize that the ethics of *iḥsān*, foundational as it is, does not on its own guarantee the establishment of a just and fair citizenship.

Hence, the problem with Taha Abderrahmane's approach is that it collapses the discourse of justice into spiritual ethics. While justice in the Islamic worldview is grounded in the believer's belief in God's ultimate justice and in devotion to Him, internal spiritual and moral drives are insufficient on their own. The Islamic legislator sets other conditions to ensure social, economic and political justice in the community. In an Islamic ethical system, justice can hardly be thought of apart from the nature of the ruling system, the conditions of the ruler and the mutual contract between the ruler and the ruled. I do not mean that Abderrahmane does not see the significance of these issues. Rather, I hold that he is inclined to think about and theorize justice and citizenship only in terms of the vertical relationship of the believer to the Creator. Even when he discusses the Islamic political system in his book *Rūh al-dīn* (*The Spirit of Religion*) – his only book devoted to political philosophy – the relationship between the ruler and the ruled and the duties of each of them are overwhelmed by the spiritualistic and moralistic discourse.

Abderrahmane's politically detached approach to justice becomes even more salient when it is juxtaposed with two of his co-citizens who examined the dialectic between ethics and politics and the impact it has on justice. The first thinker is his long-term rival Mohammed Abed al-Jabri (1935-2010) whose project the "Critique of Arab Reason" has influenced generations of researchers in the Arab world and beyond. Influential as it is, al-Jabri's critique of Arab reason suffers from methodological flaws, such as atomism and ethnocentrism, which several thinkers, including Taha Abderrahmane, rightly exposed.[48] Nonetheless, I think that al-Jabri's foray into the troubled relationship between ethics and injustice can highlight what Abderrahmane's ethics of *iḥsān* ignores.

In the fourth and last volume of his project, *al-ʿAql al-akhlāqī al-ʿarabī* (*Critique of Arab Ethical Reason*), al-Jabri embarks on an epistemological critique of the Islamic ethical tradition. Faithful to his inclination to classify, he divides Arab-Islamic ethical thought into five value systems, each revolving around a central value. The Persian ethical system was the first to disturb the homogeneity of Arab-Islamic ethical reason, and it consolidated the ethics of obedience. The second inherited ethical system was Greek ethics, and it emphasized the value of happiness (*eudaimonia*). The third imported system, according to al-Jabri, was the Sufi ethics of self-annihilation, submission and passivity. The two indigenous fourth and fifth ethical systems were Arab ethics that center on chivalry (*murū'ah*), and Islamic ethics that hinge on the value of public interest (*maṣlaḥah*). One of al-Jabri's theses in this book is that the ethics of obedience and the ethics of self-annihilation, which he ascribes to the insidious presence of the Persian and the esoteric Sufi systems of values respectively have, until the present, paradoxically co-existed with the Arabic value of chivalry and the Islamic value of public interest. Consequently, certain strands of ethical thought in the Arab-Islamic tradition have, in the guise of the devotion to God and submission to His will, perpetuated the values of obedience and submission.[49] Two salient traditions of ethical scholarly writings that al-Jabri vilifies, sometimes unjustly, are *adab* literature and works of Sufism.

Unlike al-Jabri, the relationship of some modes of Islamic ethical expression to submission and negative obedience is outside the scope of Abderrahmane's interest. Not only in his evaluation of the Islamic ethical tradition, but also in his other writings, Abderrahmane's linguistic and logical analyses eclipse the questions of power and justice. In his 1995 *Tajdīd al-manhaj fī taqwīm al-turāth* (*The Innovation of Method in the Evaluation of Tradition*), for example, he is concerned with disclosing the theological, linguistic and epistemological mechanisms of naturalization through which the Islamic tradition integrated and absorbed the ethical heritage of disparate cultures.[50] While al-Jabri traces the manifestations of discreet authoritarianism in the writings of Abū al-Ḥasan al-Amirī, al-Māwardī, Ibn Qutaybah and Ibn Miskawayh, Taha Abderrahmane works hard to demonstrate that the literary, aphoristic, theological and praxeological nature of these ethical writings are more likely to incite moral action than "dry" Greek theoretical ethics.[51] Whether the moral and spiritual value of these writings is compromised by their explicit or implicit consolidation of the status quo and the negative side of the values of obedience and submission is a problematic that does not attract his attention. As al-Jabri put it, we cannot speak about justice without killing "Khosrau" and "Annushirwan" in our tradition.[52] Al-Jabri refers to these two Persian figures as symbols of despotism because he thinks that the ethics of obedience and authoritarianism seeped into the Arab-Islamic scholarly tradition through the translation of Persian ethical literature in the early Umayyad period. That is, of course, not true! Authoritarianism is a vice that is not peculiar to any specific ethnic group.

The second Moroccan scholar that I compare with Taha Abderrahmane, Abdessalam Yassine (1928-2012), makes the same claim in even more forceful terms, but from a very different perspective. In contrast to the anti-Sufi secular ethics of al-Jabri, Yassine is an Islamist scholar whose life and thought are embedded in spiritual education. Despite the different registers of their discourse, both Taha Abderrahmane and Abdessalam Yassine place a premium on the foundational character of the ethics of *iḥsān* in Islam. For both of them, the vertical relationship between the believer and God – a relationship of love and devotion but also of modesty and fear – is the basis for all actions and relationships. Correspondingly, the two men hold that the core of Islamic ethics has been preserved in the Islamic Sufi tradition. However, Yassine, unlike Abderrahmane, is acutely sensitive to the violent political separation between ethics and politics in Islamic discursive practices. This separation, Yassine argues, has its origin in what he calls the early "historical deviation."[53] By this, he refers to the decisive moment in Islamic history when the consultative system of rule was reversed by a "biting hereditary rule" about fifty years after the death of the Prophet.[54] This historical deviation, he contends, gradually bequeathed the atomization of Islamic knowledge, the dramatic split between justice and *iḥsān*, and the conscious and unconscious perpetuation of the "religion of submission" (*dīn al-inqiyyād*) in the discursive practices of Muslims.[55] The challenge is this is how can these two halves of Islamic ontology be brought together in a postcolonial secularized culture? Thus, the reader finds in Yassine's oeuvre a smooth overlap between spiritual ethics and social and political justice, a balance that one rarely encounters in Taha Abderrahmane's works.

By referring briefly to the examples of al-Jabri and Abdessalam Yassine, my aim is to highlight that Abderrahmane's approach is oblivious to the entangled relationship between ethics and politics in Islamic thought. The outcome of his reductive conception of ethics is a failure to address the institutional realities of systems of justice. This reductive conceptualization of justice is, as I noted above, due to the exclusion of its political and historical dimensions. Abderrahmane not only skips over the political and legal conditions that are meant to guarantee justice in an Islamic society, he also theorizes the concept of justice aloof from the configurations and disfigurations of justice in Arab-Islamic intellectual discourse.[56] When detached from political considerations, the theoretical excavation into the issue of justice becomes a philosophical exercise that hovers in the sky of abstractions and ideals. As such, it both betrays the holistic nature of the spirit of justice in Islam, and it turns a blind eye to the post-Arab Spring zeitgeist wherein the Ummah is struggling for dignity and freedom.[57]

The same reductive tendency applies to Abderrahmane's reworking of the related concept of citizenship. This is a highly controversial question that cannot be settled theoretically by a few counterarguments against liberals and communitarians. Nor is the affirmation of the moral and spiritual grounds of fraternity and the priority of duty sufficient to advance a convincing discourse about citizenship in Islam. Other issues are certainly at stake.

In my view, the question of citizenship today cannot be discussed apart from serious consideration of the modern discourse on equality, rights, individual liberties and pluralism. Citizenship and the Ummah also cannot be considered apart from the modern concept and reality of the nation state and its exigencies. If the Ummah operates like a global moral entity, and its members act as "global citizens" as Abderrahmane claims, then what about the nation state? Are not individuals bound by the political and legal systems of their nation states? If so, how could the citizen of the state be reconciled with the global citizen who belongs to the Ummah? I am not suggesting that they cannot. But if we consider the main claim of Wael Hallaq in his book *The Impossible State*, the reconciliation between them is not unproblematic either. Unfortunately, Abderrahmane's politically disengaged philosophy theorizes the concept of the Ummah as if it existed in the void.

The contribution of Taha Abderrahmane to Islamic moral philosophy is without doubt innovative. What makes his contribution outstandingly significant is his critical engagement with prominent moral philosophers in the West from Rousseau and Kant to Rawls and Habermas. With these giants, he opens philosophical dialogues to reconstruct a solid theoretical ground for an Islamic ethics of purification in a terrain that is occupied by the bleak, capitalist ethics of modernity. However, Abderrahmane's inability to see beyond the confines of quietist Sufi thinking compromises his position on justice.

Endnotes

1. John Rawls, *A Theory of Justice* (revised edn. Cambridge, MA: Harvard University Press, 1999), pp.302-3.
2. Critics commonly use the designation "communitarians" or "communitarian philosophers" to refer to these philosophers: Alasdair MacIntyre (b. 1929); Michael J. Sandel (b. 1953); Charles Taylor (b. 1931); and Michael Walzer (b. 1935). These philosophers never identified themselves with the label. What they have in common is their critical response to Rawls's liberal theory of justice, and their accentuation of the decisive role of the community in shaping the individual's social identity. In this sense, they neither constitute a homogeneous movement nor did they develop any systematic philosophy that can be labeled "communitarian". Thus, the label "communitarian" in this chapter refers to the above core idea rather than any systematic philosophy. Since I am not familiar with the work of Walzer, I will mostly refer to Taylor, MacIntyre and, to a lesser extent, Sandel.
3. Taha Abderrahmane, *Rūḥ al-ḥadāthah: al-Madkhal ilā ta'sīs al-ḥadāthah al-islāmiyyah* (Casablanca: Arabic Cultural Center, 2006), p.219.
4. Abderrahmane, *Rūḥ al-ḥadāthah*, p.220.
5. Donald Dworkin, 'The Original Position', *The University of Chicago Law Review* 40(3) (Spring 1973), p.501.
6. Abderrahmane, *Rūḥ al-ḥadāthah*, p.223. In the Qur'an, there is an emphatic relationship between the concept of *taqwā* and justice (*ʿadl*). See 5:8: "Be just; that is closer to righteousness."
7. Abderrahmane, *Rūḥ al-ḥadāthah*, p.223.
8. Ibid., p.223.
9. The Covenant of Alast refers to the primordial covenant between God and human beings as stated in the Qur'an in 7:172: "And [mention] when your Lord took from the children of Adam – from their loins – their descendants and made them testify of themselves, [saying to them], 'Am I not your Lord?' They said, 'Yes, we have testified.' This is lest you should say on the day of Resurrection, 'Indeed, we were unaware of this." Taha Abderrahmane himself refers to this verse to affirm that the nature of the human being is *homo religiosus*.
10. Stephen Mulhall and Adam Swift, *Liberals and Communitarians* (2nd edn. Oxford: Blackwell, 1996), pp.3-6.
11. Azmi Bishara says: "It is no longer possible to imagine a concept of justice that does not regulate the relationship between the two principles of equality and freedom. We must seek a concept of justice, or theory if preferred, that includes affiliation groups, or identity groups, without these being at the expense of freedom and equality, but on the basis of freedom and equality." Azmi Bishara, 'On Justice in the Current Arab Context', *Tabayyun* 5 (Summer 2013), p.31.
12. One could mention a few noteworthy attempts that have been made in this respect, such as Andrew F. March, *Islam and Liberal Citizenship: The Search for an Overlapping Consensus* (Oxford: Oxford University Press, 2009); and Tariq Ramadan, *Islam and the Arab Awakening* (Oxford: Oxford University Press, 2012), p.113.
13. Abderrahmane, *Rūḥ al-ḥadāthah*, p.220.
14. Ibid., p.220.

15. Michael Sandel, *Liberalism and the Limits of Justice* (2nd edn. Cambridge: Cambridge University Press, 1998), p.60. It should be stressed that the undeniably individualistic character of Rawls's theory does not support the conclusion that the liberal citizen as Rawls conceives of him or her is self-centered and oblivious to the commitments of the community.
16. See, for example, Charles Taylor, *Philosophy and the Human Sciences: Philosophical Papers, 2* (Cambridge: Cambridge University Press, 1985), pp.187-210.
17. Abderrahmane, *Rūḥ al-ḥadāthah*, p.221; Rawls, *A Theory of Justice*, p.28.
18. Ibid., *Rūḥ al-ḥadāthah*, p.224.
19. Ibid., *Rūḥ al-ḥadāthah*, p.220.
20. Sandel, *Liberalism and the Limits of Justice,* pp.54-55, 62.
21. Alasdair MacIntyre, *After Virtue: A Study in Moral Theory* (Notre Dame: University of Notre Dame Press, 1981), pp.6-23, 226-58. For a compelling narrative of the degeneration of modern self into moral subjectivism, see Charles Taylor, *Sources of the Self: The Making* of the *Modern Identity (10th edn. Cambridge, MA:* Harvard University Press, 2001).
22. Abderrahmane, *Rūḥ al-ḥadāthah*, p.220.
23. See in the Qur'an, 2:57: "And they wronged Us not - but they were [only] wronging themselves"; 3:117: "And Allah has not wronged them, but they wrong themselves." This theological and cosmological conception of injustice to the self is discordant with Aristotle's conclusion in *Nicomachean Ethics* that a person cannot do injustice to himself.
24. Abderrahmane, *Rūḥ al-ḥadāthah*, p.232.
25. Ibid., *Rūḥ al-ḥadāthah*, p.232.
26. This idea is captured by the adage of "the priority of the right over the good." In this regard, Rawls also states that the principles of right "put limits on which satisfactions have value; they impose restrictions on what are reasonable conceptions of one's good." Rawls, *A Theory of Justice*, pp.27-28.
27. Taha Abderrahmane, *al-Haqq al-islāmī fi al-ikhtilāf al-fikrī* (Casablanca: The Arabic Cultural center, 2005), p.70; Alasdair MacIntyre, *Whose Justice? Which Rationality?* (Notre Dame: University of Notre Dame Press, 1988).
28. Taha Abderrahmane, *Su'āl al-akhlāq: musāhamah fi a-naqd al-akhlāqi li al-ḥadāthah al-gharbiyyah* (Casablanca: The Arabic Cultural Center, 2000), p.78. Charles Taylor argues along the same lines: "'the good is always primary to the right', if for no other reason because 'the good is what, in its articulation, gives the point of the rules which define the right.'" Taylor, *Sources of the Self,* p.89.
29. Wael B. Hallaq, *The Impossible State: Islam, Politics, and Modernity's Moral Predicament (New York: Columbia University Press, 2013)*,p.87.
30. Abderrahmane, *Rūḥ al-ḥadāthah*, p.221.
31. Ibid., *Rūḥ al-ḥadāthah*, p.221.
32. Ibid., *Rūḥ al-ḥadāthah*, p.221.
33. Ibid., *Rūḥ al-ḥadāthah*, p.218.
34. Taha Abderrahmane is familiar with the communitarian thinkers, and he refers to some of their works in different contexts in his books. In *Al-Haqq al-islāmī fi al-ikhtilāf al-fikrī*, he engages with Walzers' ideas about thick and thin values, and he refers in *Rūḥ al-dīn* to Charles Taylor's *The Malaise of Modernity* and *A Secular Age*, whereas in *Tajdīd al-manhaj fi taqwīm al-Turāth*, he refers to Alasdair MacIntyre's *After Virtue*. Nonetheless,

he mentions none of them nor does he refer to any of their works when he discusses the communitarians' conception of citizenship in *Rūḥ al-ḥadāthah*.

35. MacIntyre, *After Virtue*, p.263.

36. Peter McMylor, *Alasdair MacIntyre: Critic of Modernity* (New York: Routledge, 2005), p.37; Ross Poole, *Morality and Modernity* (New York: Routledge, 2005), pp.125-28.

37. Abderrahmane, *Rūḥ al-ḥadāthah*, pp.227-28.

38. Abderrahmane, *Rūḥ al-ḥadāthah*, p.228.

39. Alija Izetbegović, *Islam between East and West*, (Oak Brook, IL: American Trust Publications, 1989), pp.126-33.

40. Poole, *Morality and Modernity*, p.15.

41. For MacIntyre, his later shift to Thomism places him somewhere along the theistic view that conceives of ethical actions primarily as articulations of God's love, and not merely obligations.

42. Taylor, *Sources of the Self*, p.93.

43. Abderrahmane, *Rūḥ al-ḥadāthah*, p.228.

44. Abderrahmane, *Al-Haqq al-islāmī fi al-ikhtilāf al-fikrī*, p.153.

45. Abderrahmane, *Al-Haqq al-islāmī fi al-ikhtilāf al-fikrī*, p.174.

46. Abderrahmane's philosophy of religion can be read as a critique of the literalist and command-based conception of religion that he designates as "*akhlāq al-'i'timār*". Two manifestations of this conception of ethics in the Islamic tradition are the juristic and Salafi approaches.

47. Olivier Roy, *Secularism Confronts Islam* (trans. George Holoch, New York: Colombia University Press, 2007), p.84.

48. See, for example: Taha Abderrahmane, *Tajdīd al-manhaj fi taqwīm al-turāth* (4th edn. Casablanca: The Arabic Cultural Center, 2012), pp.19-56; and Tarabichi, *Mashākil al-ʿaql al-ʿarabī* (Beirut: Dār al-Sāqī, 1998).

49. Mohammed Abed al-Jabri, *al-ʿAql al-akhlāqī al-ʿarabī: dirāsah taḥlīliyyah naqdiyyah li nuẓum al-qiyam fi al-thaqāfah al-ʿarabiyyah* (Beirut: CAUS, 2001), pp.131-49, 427-87.

50. He calls this "pragmatic approximation" (*al-taqrīb al-tadāwulī*). Abderrahmane, *Tajdīd al-manhaj fi taqwīm al-turāth*, p.273.

51. Abderrahmane, *Tajdīd al-manhaj fi taqwīm a-turāth*, pp.390-400.

52. Al-Jabri, *Al-ʿAql al-akhlāqī al-ʿ*arabī, p.630.

53. Abdessalam Yassine, *Naẓarāt fi al-fiqh wa al-tārīkh* (Casablanca: Al-Khaṭṭābī Publishing, 1990); Abdessalam Yassine, *al-ʿAdl: al-islāmiyyūn wa al-ḥukm* (Casablanca: Al-Ufuq, 2000), pp.10, 27-29, 64.

54. Yassine, *Naẓarāt fi al-fiqh wa al-tārīkh*, pp.41, 64.

55. Yassine, *Al-ʿAdl*, pp.112-113.

56. See for example Wajih Qanssou, 'The manifestations of Justice and Liberty in the Islamic History', in *On Justice in the Arab Context* (Doha: Arab Center for Research and Policy Studies, 2014), pp.227-72.

57. Taha Abderrahmane's ideas about justice and citizenship were, of course, written in the first decade of the twenty-first century. However, he still maintains the same line of thought in all the books that he published in the aftermath of the Arab Spring, namely *Rūḥ al-dīn*; *Bu's al-dahrāniyya*; and *Su'āl al-ʿamal*.

Bibliography

Abderrahmane, Taha, *Su'āl al-akhlāq: musāhamah fī a-naqd al-akhlāqī li al-ḥadāthah al-gharbiyyah*. Casablanca: The Arabic Cultural Center, 2000.

___, *al-Ḥaqq al-islāmī fī al-ikhtilāf al-fikrī*. Casablanca: The Arabic Cultural Center, 2005.

___, *Rūḥ al-ḥadāthah: al-madkhal ilā ta'sīs al-ḥadāthah al-islāmiyyah*. Casablanca: Arabic Cultural Center, 2006.

___, *Tajdīd al-manhaj fī taqwīm al-turāth*, 4th edn. Casablanca: The Arabic Cultural Center, 2012.

Bishara, Azmi, 'On Justice in the Current Arab Context', *Tabayyun* 5 (Summer 2013), pp.1-34.

Dworkin, Donald, 'The Original Position', *The University of Chicago Law Review* 40(3) (Spring 1973), pp.500-533.

Hallaq, Wael B., *The Impossible State: Islam, Politics, and Modernity's Moral Predicament*. New York: Columbia University Press, 2013.

Izetbegović, Alija, *Islam between East and West*. Oak Brook, IL: American Trust Publications, 1989.

al-Jabri, Mohammed Abed, *al-ʿAql al-akhlāqī al-ʿarabī: dirāsah taḥlīliyyah naqdiyyah li nuẓum al-qiyam fī al-thaqāfah al-ʿarabiyyah*. Beirut: CAUS, 2001.

MacIntyre, Alasdair, *After Virtue: A Study in Moral Theory*. Notre Dame: University of Notre Dame Press, 1981.

___, *Whose Justice? Which Rationality?*. Notre Dame: University of Notre Dame Press, 1988.

March, Andrew F., *Islam and Liberal Citizenship: The Search for an Overlapping* Consensus. Oxford: Oxford University Press, 2009.

McMylor, Peter, *Alasdair MacIntyre: Critic of Modernity*. New York: Routledge, 2005.

Mulhall, Stephen, and Adam Swift, *Liberals and Communitarians*, 2nd edn. Oxford: Blackwell, 1996.

Poole, Ross, *Morality and Modernity*. New York: Routledge, 2005.

Qanssou, Wajih, 'The manifestations of Justice and Liberty in the Islamic History', in *On Justice in the Arab Context*. Doha: Arab center for Research and Policy Studies, 2014, pp.227-272.

Ramadan, Tariq, *Islam and the Arab Awakening*. Oxford: Oxford University Press, 2012.

Rawls, John, *A Theory of Justice*, revised edn, Cambridge, MA: Harvard University Press, 1999.

Roy, Olivier, *Secularism Confronts Islam*, trans. George Holoch. New York: Colombia University Press, 2007.

Sandel, Michael, *Liberalism and the Limits of Justice*, 2nd edn. Cambridge: Cambridge University Press, 1998.

Tarabichi, Georges, *Mashākil al-ʿaql al-ʿarabī*. Beirut: Dār al-Sāqī, 1998.

Taylor, Charles, *Philosophy and the Human Sciences: Philosophical Papers, 2*. Cambridge: Cambridge University Press, 1985.

___, *Sources of the Self: The Making of the Modern Identity*, 10 edn. Cambridge, MA: Harvard University press, 2001.

Yassine, Abdessalam, *Naẓarāt fī al-fiqh wa al-tārīkh*. Casablanca: Al-Khaṭṭābī Publishing, 1990.

___, *al-ʿAdl: al-islāmiyyūn wa al-ḥukm*. Casablanca: Al-Ufuq, 2000.

2

Whose Justice? When Māturīdī Meets MacIntyre

Ramon Harvey

Introduction

When Muslim intellectuals seek to engage in the great debates of the contemporary world – and the theory and practice of justice is a central one – they are caught on the horns of a dilemma. Though wanting to declare that there is a distinct Islamic notion of justice, reflecting the guidance of revelation, they also want to insist that their vision of justice is in some sense universal and able to bring Muslims into common cause with other members of society. What is needed is a kind of metatheory that can account for the way that adherents of religious traditions can engage in reasoned public debate without compromising core commitments, such as to the revealed nature of their scripture or the binding nature of its divine law.

Enter Alasdair MacIntyre. In several celebrated works, he makes a powerful argument that whereas any given tradition of enquiry can advance universal claims about justice, their justification necessarily occurs within a historically conditioned framework of thought. His work is so significant, in part, because of its role within intellectual attempts to "avoid being forced into a false choice between a contested claim for a universal moral rationality or moral relativism".[1] While MacIntyre has made transformative interventions in the field of moral philosophy, I argue that his metatheory of tradition-constituted enquiry is of moment for the contemporary articulation of a comprehensive Muslim theology.[2] This is because it gives a coherent theoretical framework for balancing the following three key ingredients in a religious tradition: the sanctity of scriptural sources; the relevance of a given intellectual tradition for reading and interpreting them; and the continuous possibility of rereading and reinterpreting them in the light of new thought and experience.

Although I will focus on the question of ethics, this cannot be divorced within Islamic tradition from the theology in which it is embedded. In my previous work on the ethical worldview of the Qur'an, I proposed that constructively building on the system of the eponymous fourth/tenth century Muslim theologian Abū Manṣūr al-Māturīdī (d. 333/944) can contribute to a contemporary theology of justice.[3] It has become almost a cliché in Islamic studies that the Māturīdite tradition, despite its historic importance for Muslim civilization, has received far less scholarly attention than the Ashʿarite or Muʿtazilite schools of thought. There are some signs that this is starting to change, including the new publication of primary sources by significant figures in the tradition and an increase in secondary literature.[4] The focus of these productions has tended to be on questions of intellectual history and, with the notable exception of mainly modern works in Turkish[5] there has been less of an attempt to discuss contemporary questions through a Māturīdite frame.

My first task in this chapter will be to provide a critical synopsis of MacIntyre's framework for staging debate between diverse traditions. Thereafter, I will briefly discuss his significant critique of modern liberal conceptions of justice, which remain a dominant force within Western thought, before moving on to outline my own approach from within the Islamic tradition. I will sketch the key features of a Māturīdite natural law theory, including the central place of God's wisdom in grounding justice on the wise purposes of the natural and divine law. Finally, I will suggest how this Islamic perspective could represent the ethical claims of its liberal counterparts, assess its own rational justification and map out a potential route to a more coherent picture of justice.

I should note that in framing my discussion in terms of opposition and debate between liberal and Islamic conceptions of justice, this chapter is pitched entirely at the level of philosophical and ethical enquiry into truth, not that of pragmatic political decision-making. This means that the question of Muslim commitment and participation within concrete liberal political orders, especially in the West, will not be broached here.[6]

MacIntyre's Tradition-constituted Enquiry

The theme of tradition-constituted enquiry has been a central plank of Alasdair MacIntyre's contribution to moral philosophy. First fully introduced as one part of the argument in his 1981 *After Virtue*, he fleshed it out considerably in its epistemological and historical dimensions in 1988's *Whose Justice? Which Rationality?*, before testing its theses yet further in 1990's *Three Rival Versions of Moral Enquiry*.[7] During the following three decades, he has continued to develop his position, including participating in collected volumes along with his critics in 1994's *After MacIntyre* and 2009's *Intractable Disputes about the Natural Law*, and writing a further related monograph, 2016's *Ethics in the Conflicts of Modernity*. The intense scrutiny that MacIntyre's work has survived prompts David Trenery's assessment that his theory of tradition-constituted enquiry is comparable in importance to that of Thomas S. Kuhn on the study of scientific revolutions.[8] In fact, he can be understood as having extended Kuhn's idea of paradigm beyond the natural sciences.

MacIntyre's thesis is that any systematic intellectual enquiry cannot proceed in abstract but must do so according to certain criteria of rationality that traditions embody in their historical development. By rationality he means the process by which ethical positions are justified through reasoned argument.[9] The use of the term "tradition" within MacIntyre's oeuvre has received some criticism in the literature for being too fluid.[10] One of the contributions of Trenery's book is clarifying some of these ambiguities. He notes that while MacIntyre dislikes giving explicit definitions on principle,[11] a careful study of his writings shows that he uses "tradition" at two levels. In common speech, a tradition is constituted by a set of beliefs and practices embodied by individuals in their lives within communities. In this sense it is – and must be – something openly accessible to ordinary people in society, a point that is important to MacIntyre as I shall elaborate below.[12] But MacIntyre's primary focus is on what he calls a tradition of enquiry, which is a metalevel of specialized intellectual activity undertaken to test, refine and justify the beliefs and practices at the first level.[13]

MacIntyre describes six stages through which a tradition in the former sense passes as it develops into a tradition in the latter sense. The first stage is comprised of beliefs, institutions and practices upon which authority is conferred, but that are not subject to systematic questioning.[14] In the second stage, this status quo is put under pressure, possibly through the emergence within the nascent tradition of rival incompatible interpretations, or the pressure exerted by foreign ideas or new circumstances.[15] The third stage consists of the emergence of reformulations and reevaluations of existing doctrine, so as to overcome the problems identified at the former level. Here, MacIntyre is careful to note in the context of religious traditions:

> Where a person or a text is assigned an authority which derives from what is taken to be their relationship to the divine, that sacred authority will be thereby in the course of this process exempt from repudiation, although its utterances may certainly be subject to reinterpretation. It is indeed one of the marks of what is taken to be sacred that it is so exempted.[16]

These three stages seem from MacIntyre's analysis to be necessarily part of tradition-constituted enquiry, such that only upon reaching the third stage would a body of activity be appropriately termed a tradition in his technical sense.[17] There are also at least three further stages that MacIntyre mentions, which represent the mature development of a tradition, though he does not so number them. The fourth stage is that of verification: the continual refinement and testing of the answers supplied by the tradition by subjecting them to dialectical questioning and the framing of objections.[18] The fifth is the institutionalization and regulation of its forms of enquiry – a methodological stage – while the sixth is the development of a theoretical account of them.[19] The later stages of the tradition are considered to be rationally superior in allowing a better correspondence between the mind and its objects.[20]

MacIntyre goes on to argue that upon reaching this level of theoretical maturity, the conception of rationality and truth within a tradition is distinguished by its initial contingent origin in a set of established beliefs and, to a certain extent, the particularities of language, alongside a given social and natural environment.[21] Inevitably there will be a number of first principles, yet these are not self-justifying. Rather, they are vindicated by their emergence in the first three stages and their survival of dialectical questioning in the fourth.[22]

Elsewhere, MacIntyre uses this idea to defend his own Thomistic position in the face of the contemporary philosophical critique that it cannot lay down indubitable first principles.[23] In fact, he turns the argument back on the Enlightenment "encyclopaedic" mode of enquiry, by arguing that its construct of a universal, impersonal rationality is undermined by the existence of alternative competing rationalities, such as the "genealogical" mode of Nietzsche, which unmasks its neutral stance as a hidden will-to-power.[24] Thus MacIntyre deploys tradition-constituted rationality to explain the incommensurability of conceptions of justice proposed by rival traditions.[25]

A crucial point follows – one that has been the cause of much misunderstanding. In MacIntyre's words:

> There is no standing ground, no place for enquiry, no way to engage in the practices of advancing, evaluating, accepting, and rejecting reasoned argument apart from that which is provided by some particular tradition or other.[26]

If understood as meaning that every human being has a contingent history, language and so forth, this is trivially true. Yet that would be to miss the point of MacIntyre's argument, which is that there is no such thing as rationality qua rationality. Anyone who tries to reach a position of pure reason fails to acknowledge the contingency of their own existence (and therefore thinking) and the need for rationality to always be embedded in a history and socially grounded within a tradition.

For MacIntyre, the social grounding of rationality is paramount because he sees it as reason giving, or justificatory, within human social interaction. He writes, "For an individual either to be or to appear rational is then for that individual to participate in the norm-governed transactions and relationships of a particular institutionalized social order."[27] MacIntyre is not here arguing for the impossibility of thought, or even kinds of reasoning, outside of traditions, but for the type of systematic enquiry involving the reciprocal justification and evaluation of arguments between individuals.[28] Another way to put this claim is that just as intellectual activity is only considered a tradition when it reaches his third stage of development, tradition-constituted enquiry only occurs from this point.

His argument is not intended to dismiss the possibility of a hypothetical lone individual engaging in advanced reasoning, such as that envisaged by Ibn Ṭufayl (d. 581/1185) in his classic thought experiment *Ḥayy b. Yaqẓān*, though it does make implausible the idea that such a person could go on to develop a systematic philosophy. The real thrust of MacIntyre's case is that, within the lived reality of the world, human beings are neither free from a social context that informs their rationality, nor can they abstract themselves from it.[29] He writes of such an imagined individual, "this may well be someone whom it is very difficult to be outside the arenas of philosophical and literary discussion."[30] MacIntyre's position is undoubtedly informed by his freely acknowledged debt to Aristotle, who remarks, "the city (*polis*) belongs to the things that exist by nature, and that man is a political animal. He who is without a city (*polis*) through nature rather than chance is either a mean sort or superior to man."[31]

MacIntyre has encountered a number of criticisms for his theory of tradition-constituted enquiry. Two central arguments made against his work are firstly that his own metatheory effectively stands outside of all traditions and thus lapses into incoherence; and secondly that it implies a profound relativity towards truth.[32] One of those to put forward the former case is Jennifer Herdt, who argues that MacIntyre's claim that there are no neutral grounds of rationality amounts to a performative self-contradiction.[33] She reads it as meaning "if anything determinate, something like 'within this particular tradition, there are no tradition-independent grounds of judgment,'"[34] which is incoherent (or at least tautological). In the collected volume *After MacIntyre*, he responds directly to this critique by elaborating on his earlier position that truth claims may be formulated universally, but their rational justification must take place within the frame of reference provided by a given tradition:[35]

> [T]here is nothing paradoxical at all in asserting that from within particular traditions assertions of universal import may be and are made, assertions formulated within the limits set by the conceptual, linguistic and argumentative possibilities of that tradition, but assertions which involve the explicit rejection of any incompatible claim, advanced in any terms whatsoever from any rival standpoint.[36]

As Trenery has argued, MacIntyre's position combines both contingent and universal elements.[37] While the term "tradition-constituted" suggests that ethical enquiry and even rationality emerge from historically grounded phenomena, he believes that the truth claims of traditions may be asserted over the domains of other traditions.[38] Moreover, he includes within this his own analysis, which seems to be a representative of his sixth "theoretical" stage. MacIntyre's claim to speak universally about tradition-constituted processes from within his own tradition is not then contradictory, though he may find it impossible to vindicate it against a rival viewpoint that does not share his starting assumptions. So, this critique of MacIntyre's metatheory of rationality collapses into the second charge, that of relativity in truth.[39]

MacIntyre deals with the problem of relativism by drawing a distinction between truth and justification. Imagine two rival traditions, each with its own claim to truth. Insofar as these claims contradict, it is only possible that one is correct, yet each sustains a justification of its claims within the framework of its own system.[40] The inference to be drawn is that at least one of the traditions is flawed, either in its first principles, its rational process, or the relationship of both to truth, however that is conceived. The problem, then, is not relativity in truth but undecidability in justification, arising from incommensurability in standards of rationality.[41]

Even should the dispute prove interminable, whereby neither side is able to win the other over to its standards, this says nothing decisive about the nature of truth and everything about the limits of rational justification. In MacIntyre's mature view, which includes his reading of the Thomist tradition, a distinction must be drawn between truth, as understood from one's own first principles, and the justification that may be found acceptable to another reasoning from shared rational premises.[42] It is only within a post-Enlightenment context that truth and reason have become so tightly bound together that what is not definitively provable on rational grounds can be so easily construed as truth-relative,[43] as many critics of MacIntyre unwittingly demonstrate.

If MacIntyre stopped at the point of elaborating radically incommensurable traditions of rationality, his perspective would still be worthy of interest. But he goes further to offer a method by which traditions can come into conversation and potentially decide points of incommensurable difference between them. This should not be too surprising, as the ability to represent their claims to each other and to enter into disagreement in the first place presupposes some commonality in translatability of language and shared logic.[44] MacIntyre argues that through familiarity with a rival tradition's modes of thought and a kind of creative empathy it is possible to fairly represent its claims. In fact, one of the obvious achievements of MacIntyre's own work is his skill in animating the various traditions that act as his protagonists.

From this point, a number of dialectical engagements are possible: moving over to the new tradition (as MacIntyre himself did in embracing Aristotelianism and then Thomism);[45] rationally defeating it; or even synthesizing a third tradition from the two. In this latter case, he gives the example of Aquinas, who was simultaneously fluent in the Augustinian and Aristotelian traditions of his time, and thus able to combine them in Thomism.[46]

It is in this distinctive idea of direct interaction between rival traditions of reason that MacIntyre makes his strongest case against relativism and sets the stage for my preliminary engagement with the liberal perspective from an Islamic tradition of justice, which is the ultimate purpose of this chapter.

MacIntyre argues that one tradition is able to vindicate itself vis-à-vis another with respect to rationality by a demonstration of its superior rational resources.[47] It does this by reformulating the predicament of its opponent in its own terms to solve problems that were insoluble from the rival tradition's perspective. In his words:

> For among those resources, so it is claimed, is an ability not only to identify as limitations, defects, and errors of the opposing view what are or ought to be taken to be limitations, defects, and errors in the light of the standards of the opposing view itself, but also to explain in precise and detailed terms what it is about the opposing view which engenders just these particular limitations, defects and errors and also what it is about that view which must deprive it of the resources required for understanding, overcoming, and correcting them.[48]

Within his works, MacIntyre gives examples meant to show that from the perspective of his Thomistic tradition, various other intellectual traditions may be rationally defeated in this way.[49] But he also presents a scenario in which, despite having apparently demonstrated this superiority with respect to rationality from within his tradition, a rival – he uses utilitarianism – would be unwilling to accept defeat due to its radically different first principles.[50]

It is for this reason that Gerald McKenny argues that perhaps MacIntyre is not entirely successful in avoiding a kind of relativism. He points out that MacIntyre's theory requires a given tradition to be epistemologically open to the resources provided by its rival, yet there is no reason from within the first tradition to abandon those of its own standards that preclude this alternative perspective. McKenny observes that if two traditions reach an impasse that they are unable to resolve through shared rational enquiry, then the moral world is relativized in practice, even if not in theory.[51] I would argue, however, that this point all but vindicates MacIntyre's case. If he succeeds in setting out a consistent theory by which rival traditions may dialectically judge the strength of their rationally held positions and he is able to provide examples of how such debates have occurred in history, it is to his credit. It is unfair to burden him with resolving all moral difference.

Rather, it seems sufficient that he shows that it is possible in principle for adherents of diverse traditions to empathically appreciate and accept the rational superiority of their counterparts.

Another argument that can be raised against MacIntyre is that he fails to account for the power dynamics at play in the history of ethical debate. A school of thought does not succeed merely by rationally defeating its rivals, but for a host of reasons, including considerations of politics.[52] MacIntyre, an erstwhile Marxist, is well aware of the importance of material circumstances in history, though it is fair to say that he emphasizes the impact of rational debate at their expense in his mature period. This point does not undercut his theory of tradition-constituted enquiry, however, as he can argue that a certain tradition, such as his own Thomism, or NeoAristotelianism, can become eclipsed within a certain geographical and historical space without thereby losing the argument on rational grounds. A large part of MacIntyre's argument in *After Virtue* is devoted to the stages by which an Aristotelian virtue ethics, despite its superiority, became eclipsed within the Western ethical tradition.[53] In many ways, his later Gifford Lectures, which became *Three Rival Versions of Moral Enquiry*, can be psychologically read as MacIntyre rerunning the core debates and showing that Aristotelian Thomists had the moral victory.

If MacIntyre's method is admitted as a possible frame for an engagement between conceptions of justice in the liberal and Islamic traditions, it is necessary to provide an outline of each one and to identify the major points of incommensurability between them. This will be the subject of the next two sections.

MacIntyre's Analysis of Justice in the Liberal Tradition

In *Whose Justice? Which Rationality?* MacIntyre tackles the question of justice in liberalism directly, treating the liberal tradition as a distinct tradition of enquiry with its own standards of justification.[54] He does not, however, give it as much attention as the other traditions he analyzes, instead painting broad brushstrokes.[55] More sustained critical treatment of the liberal tradition, especially the notion of the secular, has been provided by figures who have engaged with MacIntyre's contributions to the field, such as Talal Asad and Charles Taylor.[56] As this essay is only a preliminary attempt to use MacIntyre's ideas to consider the case of liberal and Māturīdite theories of justice, it is useful to add to the previous section by sketching his assessment of liberalism. A full engagement with liberal thought would require considerably more attention to a full array of its representatives and critics.

One of MacIntyre's main claims, substantiated by his discussion of liberalism, is that a tradition's standards of justice are subordinated to the rational framework in which they are embedded. The liberal tradition of rationality, which arguably goes back through Hobbes to the Ancient Greek Sophists, explains social action through the present aims and interests of individuals, rather than a teleological ordering, as understood by Aristotle, Aquinas and al-Māturīdī, in which the good is ontologically prior to individual desires.[57] MacIntyre argues that liberalism transposes the individual's nature as a customer within the marketplace into rational enquiry.[58] That is, the good is privatized and each individual seeks their own good in diverse aspects of their life and, in doing so, ranks their preferences as follows:

> I want it to be the case that such and such; Doing so and so will enable me to achieve its being the case that such and such; There is no other way of so enabling me which I prefer; Doing so and so will not frustrate any equal or stronger preference.[59]

From this perspective, individuals may argue for a range of principles by which justice is to be achieved within society and by some form of aggregation these shape the socio-moral landscape. The liberal order, however, in being opposed to any single conception of the good that supervenes upon all aspects of human life, allows no position to win against the others.[60] All that the various philosophical debates of social contractarians, utilitarians, Marxists and Kantians amount to is better clarification of the commitments engendered by their starting assumptions, not a method by which to choose one rather than another.[61] It is perhaps for this reason that MacIntyre does not provide a detailed analysis of the variations between them; his purpose is to demonstrate that they are different aspects of one tradition, which relies upon a single form of rationality.

MacIntyre draws several conclusions from this, which he ranks within levels. First, there is no substantive agreement about what justice is to consist of within the liberal order as there is no consensus on human good.[62] Second, despite their differences, the diverse approaches to justice within liberalism are predicated on a shared conception of a liberal individual of a certain rational stamp; one who chooses which ethical theory is preferable just as they engage in ranking preferences in other parts of their life.[63]

Third, within the "marketplace of ideas", justice, which cannot be definitively settled, becomes a matter of ensuring equality in terms of one's ability to take a place at the bargaining table and to put forward preferences to be accounted in whatever form of aggregation is successful.[64] Fourth, that the ultimate appeal to justice is within a legal system that may, on occasion, invoke any of the philosophical positions deemed acceptable within the liberal sphere – as there is no settled idea of human good to be used as a standard. MacIntyre comments, "The lawyers, not the philosophers, are the clergy of liberalism."[65]

Finally, and perhaps ironically, the liberal order's public insistence that there is no good to human life, but rather just the preferences of individuals within its political, social and economic spheres, amounts to the hidden position that this good is, in effect, nothing other than the perpetuation of the very order that offers these choices.[66] Therefore, even though liberalism is unable to coherently articulate a single principle for justice, it institutionalizes the ongoing debate over its constitution and ensures that it takes place on liberal terms. Although not mentioned by MacIntyre here, these terms include a rejection of any appeal to phenomena that lie outside the post-Enlightenment criteria for rationally admissible public evidence, such as reference to God, religious scripture, or spiritual inspiration.[67]

This is a key point in debating justice with the Islamic tradition from the liberal perspective. An avowed liberal would surely argue that the best opportunity to secure justice is on the basis of a universal reason that is assumed to be extended equally to all individuals without appeal to traditional authority.[68] This reflects a tendency within liberalism to implicitly exclude what is distinctively religious from the question of public morality, as has long been the case in the Christian tradition.[69] Therefore, any Islamic standard of justice faces an immediate credibility problem in the West: if Christian claims appealing to the religious and moral heritage are treated with skepticism, *a fortiori* Muslim ones will be.

A potential solution to this problem has been proposed by John Rawls through his notion of a political liberalism that claims to allow multiple incompatible comprehensive theories of the good to co-exist based on an "overlapping consensus".[70] This would, in theory, allow the adherents of various traditions to come to agreement on basic points of political order. But for the scheme to work, Rawls requires the adherents of various traditions to be "reasonable", meaning that they justify their views in a manner that other free and equal citizens could also accept.[71] Thus, Rawls's scheme is based on finding a solution to the problem of how various traditions can reach political consensus within a preexisting liberal order via a distinctively liberal form of rationality. Notably, within the limits of this practical proposal, Mohammad Fadel argues that the theological resources of Islam do potentially allow a Muslim to "reconcile her normative commitments to Islam as a comprehensive theory of the good and her political commitments to a liberal constitutional order."[72]

The purpose of this chapter, however, is not to deal with commitments predicated on the dominance of the liberal political order, but to explore the underlying philosophical debates about the nature of justice that may, from a different theory of the good, even put such an order into question. The power of MacIntyre's analysis is to undermine the assumed neutrality of liberal rationality and to reveal its disguised societal will-to-power. He not only annuls its philosophical priority by exposing it to the cut and thrust of tradition-constituted enquiry, but astutely particularizes this general conclusion to assert that no other perspective can take on the mantle of a neutral arbiter of value.

Justice in the Māturīdite Tradition

As with liberalism, the broad category of Islamic tradition precedes the specific theories of justice that may be articulated from within it.[73] This means that mapping the main frameworks of rationality that provide resources for tradition-constituted enquiry is a useful starting point. Here, Sherman Jackson explodes the standard dichotomy within study of Islamic history between so-called Rationalism and Traditionalism. He proposes that rather than the use of reason, or the lack thereof, being central to characterizing the difference between them, both theological tendencies embody distinct regimes of reason. He argues that the approach taken by the rational theologians (*mutakallimūn*) draws on the Aristotelian-Neoplatonic tradition as a discursive way of thinking about revelation, whereas the Traditionalists (*ahl al-ḥadīth*) – represented foremost by collectors and compilers of prophetic traditions – rely on a continuous, informal, selective endorsement of revealed and traditional material in the light of new ideas.[74]

The kind of rational justification required by a MacIntyrean engagement between traditions makes the former "Rationalist" mode of Muslim theology a more attractive prospect for the present task. Three major traditions within Islamic theological history are particularly significant: the Muʿtazilites, the Ashʿarites and the Māturīdites.[75] Though these theological schools differ on key metaethical questions bearing on social justice, at the level of fundamental reason their selective appropriation of aspects of the rational framework of Aristotelian-Neoplatonic thought at MacIntyre's second and third stages of tradition makes them more similar to each other (and to MacIntyre's own Thomistic perspective) than to the varieties of liberal thought entertained in the modern philosophy department.

In the remainder of this chapter, I will build upon my own prior study of Qur'anic social justice in the light of Māturīdite theology, especially its eponymous figure Abū Manṣūr al-Māturīdī, to outline the major aspects of a Māturīdite theory of justice.[76] I suggest that this perspective has the potential to emerge as a credible participant in debate with other traditions, including the liberal perspectives discussed in the previous section. Despite undergoing development in the course of its history, the Māturīdite tradition has disguised the historicity of its own genesis – as such traditions tend to do – thereby typically attributing its entire theological repertoire to its eponym or even beyond him to the early Iraqī theologian Abū Ḥanīfah (d. 150/767).[77] In the theoretical language of tradition-constituted enquiry, it seemingly has not hitherto become fully self-conscious of its own reformulations, refinements and methodological institutionalization, meaning that it has not reached MacIntyre's sixth stage.[78]

To speak of Māturīdism in this way requires an acknowledgment that theology is a human construct.[79] While the theory I put forward will draw from the earlier school tradition, it must necessarily be a contemporary approach to theology, a so-called *kalām jadīd*.[80] Just as the rational position of al-Māturīdī emerged from engagement with the data of revelation in an Aristotelian-Neoplatonic milieu, my rereading of this tradition attempts to frame it within a theoretical account of its own processes of moral enquiry as developed by figures such as MacIntyre. It could be called "neo-Māturīdism" to signify this self-reflexive approach, as well as its debt to the world of contemporary thought that any credible theology must engage.[81] This would recall, yet interestingly contrast with, the more common "neo-Muʿtazilite" epithet given to a number of modern Muslim thinkers who favour a return to rational thinking in a manner that they claim is reminiscent of the Muʿtazilites.[82]

The concept of justice in Māturīdite thought is inextricably linked to God's wisdom (*ḥikmah*). This identification is found in al-Māturīdī's *Kitāb al-tawḥīd* in unambiguous terms: "The explanation of wisdom is 'hitting the mark', which is putting everything in its place; that is the meaning of justice and His action does not divert from it."[83] Considering this explanatory gloss – which bases God's justice on His wisdom – in the context of al-Māturīdī's theological system, there is no attribute beyond God's wisdom that regulates what the "place" for everything in creation should be. His eternal wisdom is given equal status to His omniscience, whereby He cannot be ignorant, and His self-sufficiency, which precludes Him acting for a personal benefit of any kind.[84] The distinctive focus of al-Māturīdī on the attribute of wisdom has been noticed in the literature and its sources and implications deserve further investigation.[85]

The Māturīdite approach to justice within human society is thus based on a number of metaphysical postulates flowing from God who creates a contingent world, the natural moral properties within it (natural law), and the supernatural communication of revelation (divine law). God's eternal attribute of wisdom (*ḥikmah*) is identified as the basic source of all three aspects of reality.[86] Thus, the world contains signs that point to the wisdom of its Creator, including the existence of morality, which is naturally accessible to human beings,[87] and the distinctive messages sent with prophets that provide corroboration and a further extension of these truths.[88] If life within the world can furnish the human being with knowledge of the existence of God and a moral code, then the natural law is to be treated, in principle, as authoritative over all people.[89] What are the limits of the natural law from a Māturīdite perspective? My approach is to treat both the code of basic moral rules (*aḥkām*; sing. *ḥukm*) and the principles underlying them (*ḥikmahs*) as potentially discoverable via experience and reflection.[90] But the application of these rules and principles to particular cases is not known with certainty and requires a process of deliberation and the development of practical wisdom in the person of the moral agent, ideally supported by the guidance of revelation.

The divine law, as found in the Qur'an and Sunnah of the Prophet Muhammad, goes beyond the natural law in several respects. First, it deals with matters of worship that are not rationally determinable, for instance the number of ritual prayers to be performed per day. Secondly, the divine law provides rulings that make the *ḥikmah*s of the law operative within a specific prophetic community. Such dispensations of the Shariᶜah (divine law and moral code) have a long history prior to the Prophet Muhammad, who brings the culminating revealed intervention in human history. As such, his Shariᶜah can abrogate the laws – though not the underlying moral principles – within the Torah of Moses and the Evangel of Jesus.[91]

Insofar as a shariᶜah is revealed to a prophet, and applied to situations he deals with, it is not subject to doubt or amendment by human agents. But according to the present theory, the rightness of a prophet's shariᶜah is predicated on its goodness read as an objective moral quality; it varies between revealed dispensations precisely because the manner by which the good can be realised may shift with time and place.[92] Another way to put this point is that the *ḥikmah*s of the law are the causes that God assigns to bring their associated rules into existence.[93] Thus, it is a teleological system such that performance of right action can only be understood within a metaphysical context of beneficial and wise purposes.

The question of how the law is to be understood after the lifetime of the Prophet Muhammad is one for which the present Māturīdite reading offers a challenge to prevailing classical approaches to legal theory. Al-Māturīdī states that it is possible for *ijtihād* (exhaustive legal enquiry) or *ijmāᶜ* (consensus) to determine when the cause of a Qur'anic rule is not present and so its associated rule is abrogated, even after the period of revelation.[94] Once it is appreciated that *naskh* (abrogation) does not just refer to God's repeal of one law by another, but also the juristic tool used to determine the decreed expiration times of rulings,[95] such a position is not inherently implausible.[96] Moreover, within such a framework, a rule abrogated when its wisdom is not met can be reinstated when it is once more or can be replaced by a more suitable rule. One of the roles of the ulema, according to this conception, is to use their expert knowledge to not only clarify – at the level of rules – how the multivariate texts of the Qur'an and Sunna are to be understood and apparent conflicts reconciled, but to check the application of their underlying principles to the ever-changing world.

Where does justice come in? On the social level, it is the ideal wise purpose (*ghāyah*, or *telos*) to which the *ḥikmah*s of the natural and divine law collectively lead.[97] Theologically, each of these principles can be read as the created effect of eternal divine wisdom, meaning that the just society is one that fully embodies the providential good order of its creator. As within the Qur'anic picture, life in the world is meant as a test of human excellence.[98]

Even if it may be very difficult, or impossible, to realise justice in the world, it is the duty of humanity to pursue it.

Vital to this effort is the role of the personal moral agency of individual human beings who act with justice in their daily interactions. One of the most important qualities that each person should inculcate is *ḥikmah*, in the sense of practical wisdom. This allows one to attain the wise purposes of the natural and divine law, which are founded in God's attribute of *ḥikmah*. Within a virtue ethics framework, it can be considered a principal good, as mentioned in the Qur'anic verse 2:269, "[God] gives wisdom to whomsoever He wishes and the one who is given wisdom has received abundant good."[99] Moreover, just as was mentioned above in relation to the natural law, the divine law no less requires practical decision-making by every responsible agent in their application of moral and legal rules to the diverse circumstances of life.[100] Unlike an approach to Islamic law in which jurists are expected to deduce a specific *ḥukm* for every conceivable situation in a person's life – the stereotype is an abdication of moral responsibility by continually turning to a mufti, or jurisconsult, for a *fatwā* (legal opinion) – the just individual is meant to develop the ability to judge how the rules and principles of the Shariʿah relate to their diverse experiences.[101] In fact, notwithstanding the importance of expert jurists for specialised intellectual work, such an approach is much closer to the original meaning of the word *fiqh* as *fahm* (understanding), than its later technical translation as "jurisprudence" for a discipline accessible only to an elite class of ulema.

What, then, would a Māturīdite theology make of the liberal tradition's conception(s) of justice? According to MacIntyre's metatheory, if the rational standards of two traditions are incommensurable, then the first would have to be able to explain not only the limitations of the second's view, but why its rival is unable to overcome them within its own rational framework. But, as discussed above, this only amounts to a rational defeat if the rival tradition would see it in these terms. Could Māturīdism push liberalism into a state of epistemic crisis? To do so, it would have to work from its own first principles to systematically unmask liberalism's failure to provide a rationally satisfying account of the good.

I will now draw on MacIntyre's critique of liberalism to suggest a line of argument that could be pursued. As discussed in the previous section, liberalism adopts the stance of a consumer seeking personal preferences and so is always in the business of ranking various conflicting desires, duties, or contractual obligations relating to the different aspects of human life. Its rejection of a teleological view means that it can never look at the individual, let alone the society, as serving a greater moral purpose. The Māturīdite perspective could argue that this lack of a single conception of the good in human life is a hollowness at the core of liberalism in stark contrast to its own vision of unified meaning through participation in the wisdom of the divine. Thus, while the liberal paradigm is unable to provide a global theory to account for moral intuitions about justice, the Māturīdite view could argue these intuitions arise consistently from natural law based on a higher, purposeful wisdom.[102] This arguably would leave liberalism exposed to an epistemic crisis that can be diagnosed and treated with resources from within the Islamic tradition.

Conclusion

My main aim in this chapter has been twofold: to demonstrate the possibility of using a MacIntyrean metatheory to stage an engagement between Islamic and liberal conceptions of justice and to outline the specific Islamic ethical theory that I think can best undertake this task. I have argued that despite a range of valuable critiques over the past decades, many of which have helped MacIntyre refine his views, the basic notion of tradition-constituted enquiry has emerged unscathed as a useful tool for debate between radically different traditions of rationality and ethics. Though it has been able to withstand the critique that it collapses into relativism, it is less clear that the engagement between those with different first principles will always result in a decisive victory for a single tradition.

In the arena of debate between conceptions of justice, MacIntyre's critique of the liberal tradition may be a way to move beyond the unresolvable contestation between its vying theories. In his entry in the *Stanford Encyclopedia of Philosophy*, David Miller implicitly confirms MacIntyre's conclusion that none of the contemporary liberal philosophical options provide a comprehensive treatment of considered convictions about justice in all the various facets of human life.[103]

I have proposed that a Māturīdite perspective is able to stand in one of the great traditions of Muslim rational theology while also benefiting from the diverse perspectives available within modern thought. Sherman Jackson comments on the possible utility of the Māturīdite standpoint for Muslim theology in the West as follows: "it may constitute the untried theological panacea that is firmly grounded in and identified with Sunni Tradition."[104] In terms of conceiving of justice from within this tradition, I have sketched the main principles upon which it can be constituted as an ethical theory, which involve the concept of God's wisdom and its relevance to natural and divine law. I then provided some initial reflections on the terms in which such a theory could attempt to engage the liberal tradition and to provoke an epistemic crisis.

It is not obvious that proponents of liberalism would, in practice, accept rational defeat from those debating with an Islamic ethical framework, notwithstanding that such a refusal would likely reflect factors transcending rational argumentation alone. It may be that MacIntyre's Thomistic – or as he now prefers – NeoAristotelian tradition would have more success by showing, as he has himself endeavored to do in his career, that the liberal tradition is composed of dislocated fragments from its own moral framework.[105] Perhaps the more productive engagement for Islamic thought would be with such a fellow theistic tradition committed to the natural law. But in that case does the conversation have to be framed only in competitive and antagonistic terms?

I have now returned to the initial question of how Muslims can hold on to their particular tradition-constituted conception of justice yet act in concert with others. According to the present argument, the practical moral rules and principles of natural law should be the standard that Muslims require other traditions to uphold and the basis on which they build collaborative platforms. This shared approach may manifest most easily with theists who ground their moral vision within a scriptural tradition, though it should here be emphasized that, in general, the rulings prescribed by the Islamic dispensation of divine law would only be treated as binding upon members of the Muslim community.[106]

Of course, philosophical interaction will necessarily also be broached with those, such as adherents of liberalism, who do not accept the precepts, or the underlying theology, of the natural law as formulated within an Islamic theory of justice. It is here that the MacIntyrean framework remains an important method for empathetic engagement that may result in greater mutual appreciation of the alternative rationalities grounding diverse moral intuitions about justice.

Endnotes

1. Rufus Black, review of 'Lawrence S. Cunningham (ed.), *Intractable Disputes about the Natural Law: Alasdair MacIntyre and Critics* (Notre Dame, IN: University of Notre Dame Press, 2009)', in *Studies in Christian Ethics* 24(2) (May, 2011), p.251. See also pp.251-53.
2. Sherman Jackson parallels many of MacIntyre's insights in his account of traditions of theological rationality within Islamic civilization. See Sherman Jackson, *Islam and the Problem of Black Suffering* (Oxford: Oxford University Press, 2009), pp.27-45. Also relevant is the work of Talal Asad. See Ovamir Anjum, 'Islam as a Discursive Tradition: Talal Asad and His Interlocutors', *Comparative Studies of South Asia, Africa and the Middle East* 27(3) (2007), pp.662-63. But whereas Asad mainly develops MacIntyre in an anthropological direction, I am interested in the philosophical dimensions of his work.
3. Ramon Harvey, *The Qur'an and the Just Society* (Edinburgh: Edinburgh University Press, 2018), p.194. Cf. Fazlur Rahman, *Revival and Reform in Islam: A Study of Islamic Fundamentalism* (Oxford: Oneworld, 2000), pp.61-63.
4. See Sabine Schmidtke, 'Introduction', in *The Oxford Handbook of Islamic Theology*, ed. Sabine Schmidtke (Oxford: Oxford University Press, 2016), pp.14-15; Angelika Brodersen, 'New Light on the Emergence of Māturīdism: Abū Shakūr al-Sālimī (Fifth/Eleventh Century) and his *Kitāb al-tamhīd fī bayan al-tawḥīd*', *Journal of Islamic Studies*, 31(3) (2020), pp.332-34.
5. See Philip Dorroll, 'Modern by Tradition: Abū Manṣūr al-Māturīdī and the New Turkish Theology', PhD dissertation (Emory University, 2013), pp.234-85. This has now been superseded by Dorroll's book *Islamic Theology in the Turkish Republic* (Edinburgh: Edinburgh University Press, 2021). For a systematic explication of Māturīdite theology in conversation with contemporary theology and philosophy, see Ramon Harvey, *Transcendent God, Rational World: A Māturīdī Theology* (Edinburgh: Edinburgh University Press, 2021).
6. For detailed discussion of these points, see Mohammad Fadel, 'The True, the Good and the Reasonable: The Theological and Ethical Roots of Public Reason in Islamic Law', *Canadian Journal of Law and Jurisprudence* 21(1) (2008), pp.1-65.
7. A fourth work, *Dependent Rational Animals*, published in 1999, makes a revamped case for the biological "nature" of humankind, a key part of his defence of a Thomistic natural law theory. Though important for MacIntyre's wider system, it has much less to say about his metatheory of tradition-constituted enquiry, which is the focus of this section. See Alasdair MacIntyre, *Dependent Rational Animals: Why Human Beings Need the Virtues* (Chicago: Carus, 1999), pp.5-9; David Trenery, *Alasdair MacIntyre, George Lindbeck, and the Nature of Tradition* (Eugene, OR: Wipf and Stock Publishers, 2014), pp.91-92.
8. Trenery, *Alasdair MacIntyre*, p.244. MacIntyre highlights the impact that reading and direct encounter with Kuhn made on his thinking. Alasdair MacIntyre, *The Tasks of Philosophy: Selected Essays, Volume 1* (Cambridge: Cambridge University Press, 2006), pp.vii-viii.
9. See Alasdair MacIntyre, *Whose Justice? Which Rationality?* (London: Duckworth, 1988), pp.2-5.
10. See the articles quoted in Trenery, *Alasdair MacIntyre*, pp.181-82.
11. Trenery, *Alasdair MacIntyre*, p.182. See MacIntyre, *Whose Justice? Which Rationality?*, p.10.

12. MacIntyre's personal investment in his project may be connected to the stages of development in his own commitments. It is conceivable that his grand narrative of ethical thought reflects his intellectual journey as a Presbyterian, Marxist, Aristotelian and finally Thomist/NeoAristotelian. See Peter McMylor, 'Marxism and Christianity: Dependencies and Differences in Alasdair MacIntyre's Critical Social Thought', *Theoria* 55(116) (2008), p.47. See also Trenery, *Alasdair MacIntyre*, pp.6-9, 57-59.
13. Trenery, *Alasdair MacIntyre*, pp.184-85.
14. MacIntyre, *Whose Justice? Which Rationality?*, p.354.
15. MacIntyre, *Whose Justice? Which Rationality?*, pp.354-55; MacIntyre, *The Tasks of Philosophy*, p.12.
16. MacIntyre, *Whose Justice? Which Rationality?*, p.355.
17. On this point, see also Jackson, *Islam and the Problem of Black Suffering*, p.42.
18. Compare in the context of Islamic tradition with Sherman Jackson, *On the Boundaries of Theological Tolerance in Islam: Abū Ḥāmid al-Ghāzalī's* Fayṣal al-Tafriqa Bayna al-Islām wa al-Zandaqa (Oxford: Oxford University Press, 2002), pp.9-10.
19. MacIntyre, *Whose Justice? Which Rationality?*, pp.358-59.
20. MacIntyre, *Whose Justice? Which Rationality?*, pp.356-57. See Jean Porter, 'Tradition in the Recent Work of Alasdair MacIntyre', in *Alasdair MacIntyre*, ed. Mark C. Murphy (Cambridge: Cambridge University Press, 2003), p.47.
21. MacIntyre, *Whose Justice? Which Rationality?*, pp.360-61.
22. MacIntyre, *Whose Justice? Which Rationality?*, p.360.
23. Alasdair MacIntyre, 'First Principles, Final Ends, and Contemporary Philosophical Issues', in *The MacIntyre Reader*, ed. Kelvin Knight (Notre Dame, IN: University of Notre Dame Press, 1998), pp.171, 186-87.
24. Alasdair MacIntyre, *Three Rival Versions of Moral Enquiry: Encyclopaedia, Genealogy, and Tradition: Being Gifford Lectures Delivered in the University of Edinburgh in 1988* (London: Duckworth, 1990), pp.35, 42-43.
25. MacIntyre, *Whose Justice? Which Rationality?*, p.350.
26. MacIntyre, *Whose Justice? Which Rationality*, p.350. Trenery also highlights the importance of MacIntyre's engagement with the hermeneutics of Hans-Georg Gadamer in developing this position, a point that he has acknowledged. Trenery, *Alasdair MacIntyre*, p.107. Cf. Hans-Georg Gadamer, *Truth and Method* (London and New York: Bloomsbury, 2013), p.293-94.
27. Alasdair MacIntyre, 'Practical Rationalities as Forms of Social Structure', in *The MacIntyre Reader*, ed. Kelvin Knight (Notre Dame, IN: University of Notre Dame Press, 1998), pp.120-21. Cf. Jackson, *Islam and the Problem of Black Suffering*, p.44.
28. MacIntyre, *Whose Justice? Which Rationality?*, p.367.
29. See MacIntyre, *Dependent Rational Animals*, p.74.
30. MacIntyre, 'Practical Rationalities as Forms of Social Structure', p.135.
31. Aristotle, *The Politics*, trans. Carnes Lord (Chicago, IL: University of Chicago Press, 1984), p.37. See Thomas L. Pangle and Timothy W. Burns, *The Key Texts of Political Philosophy: An Introduction* (Cambridge: Cambridge University Press, 2014), p.163.
32. See Trenery, *Alasdair MacIntyre*, p.125.
33. Herdt correctly represents MacIntyre as making the qualified claim that his failure to find a neutral ground for rationality is evidence that it does not exist. Jennifer A. Herdt, 'Alasdair MacIntyre's "Rationality of Traditions" and Tradition-Transcendental Standards

of Justification', *The Journal of Religion* 78(4) (October 1998), p.527. His position is that the failure of liberalism to provide a neutral tradition-independent ground for assessing the claims of traditions is the strongest possible evidence against such a ground existing. MacIntyre, *Whose Justice? Which Rationality*, p.346.

34. Herdt, 'Alasdair MacIntyre's "Rationality of Traditions"', p.527.

35. MacIntyre, *Whose Justice? Which Rationality*, p.9.

36. Alasdair MacIntyre, 'A Partial Response to My Critics', in *After MacIntyre: Critical Perspectives on the Work of Alasdair MacIntyre*, eds. John Horton and Susan Mendes (Notre Dame, IN: University of Notre Dame Press, 1994), p.295.

37. Specifically, he contends MacIntyre combines tradition-specific aspects of incommensurability and incompatible standards of justification with universalist aspects of logical consistency and epistemological openness. Trenery, *Alasdair MacIntyre*, p.129.

38. MacIntyre, *The Tasks of Philosophy*, pp.10-11.

39. Herdt goes on to argue that MacIntyre's theory of conflict resolution between traditions, put forward to avoid the charge of relativism, leads him into a bind: either it succeeds, but as a tradition-independent method, thus contradicting his claims, or it fails, and leaves him in a position of relativism. Herdt, 'Alasdair MacIntyre's "Rationality of Traditions"', p.527. My judgement, for reasons given in this chapter, is that MacIntyre's theory provides a viable way for incommensurable traditions to debate without becoming tradition independent or relativistic.

40. MacIntyre, *Three Rival Versions of Moral Enquiry*, p.43.

41. MacIntyre, 'A Partial Response to My Critics', p.295. Elsewhere, he argues against the pragmatist challenge that "truth is to be identified with idealized justification." Alasdair MacIntyre, 'Moral Relativism, Truth and Justification', in *The MacIntyre Reader*, ed. Kelvin Knight (Notre Dame, IN: University of Notre Dame Press, 1998), p.206. See pp.205-07.

42. Alasdair MacIntyre, 'Intractable Moral Disagreements', in *Intractable Disputes about the Natural Law*, ed. Lawrence S. Cunningham (Notre Dame, IN: University of Notre Dame Press, 2009), pp.34-35.

43. See Sherman Jackson, 'Not Truth But Tolerance: A (Much Belated) Response to Atif Khalil', *American Journal of Islamic Social Sciences (AJISS)* 28(4) (2011), p.151.

44. MacIntyre, *Whose Justice? Which Rationality?*, p.351. See Trenery, *Alasdair MacIntyre*, p.132. At least from MacIntyre's Thomistic perspective, any systematic enquiry presupposes the laws of logic. Pangle and Burns, *The Key Texts of Political Philosophy*, p.157. But Porter astutely points out that MacIntyre has not fully attempted to discuss the interaction of traditions that are not closely related in genealogy. Porter, 'Tradition in the Recent Work of Alasdair MacIntyre', p.55.

45. See Alasdair MacIntyre, *After Virtue: A Study in Moral Theory* (3rd edn. Notre Dame, IN: University of Notre Dame Press, 2007), pp.x-xi.

46. MacIntyre, *Three Rival Versions of Moral Enquiry*, pp.114-15. MacIntyre also gives the example of Descartes becoming the first Cartesian. MacIntyre, *Whose Justice? Which Rationality?*, p.360. Jackson describes the famous conversion of al-Ashʿarī from the Muʿtazilites to begin his own theological synthesis. Jackson, *Islam and the Problem of Black Suffering*, p.79.

47. MacIntyre, 'A Partial Response to My Critics', p.297.

48. MacIntyre, *Three Rival Versions of Moral Enquiry*, p.146.

49. *Whose Justice? Which Rationality?*, pp.361-65; MacIntyre, 'A Partial Response to My

Critics', pp.295-97; MacIntyre, 'Moral Relativism, Truth and Justification', pp.216-20.
50. MacIntyre, 'Intractable Moral Disagreements', pp.50-51. Utilitarianism, as MacIntyre characterizes it, requires a starting point in a conception of human happiness (or another concept to replace it) to explain the purpose of following moral rules. But, as opposed to the Aristotelian, the utilitarian, by definition, abstracts this notion as a psychological state from particular ends embodying the good. See MacIntyre, 'Intractable Moral Disagreements', pp.44-49.
51. Gerald McKenny, 'Moral Disagreement and the Limits of Reason: Reflections on MacIntyre and Ratzinger', in *Intractable Disputes about the Natural Law*, ed. Lawrence S. Cunningham (Notre Dame, IN: University of Notre Dame Press, 2009), pp.211-13.
52. Thanks to Ovamir Anjum for this point of critique. The same line of argument can be found in Wael B. Hallaq, *Restating Orientalism: A Critique of Modern Knowledge* (New York: Columbia University Press, 2018), p.141.
53. See MacIntyre, *After Virtue: A Study in Moral Theory*, pp.226-36.
54. MacIntyre, *Whose Justice? Which Rationality?*, pp.326-48. This may seem at odds with his earlier characterization of the individualistic aspect of liberalism, which he opposes to the prior Aristotelian tradition. MacIntyre, *After Virtue*, pp.250-52. In an interview, MacIntyre clarifies that he distinguishes between the anti-traditional tendency of liberalism and the emergence of a distinct tradition of liberal enquiry embodied in certain thinkers and their texts. Alasdair MacIntyre, 'An Interview for *Cogito*', in *The MacIntyre Reader*, ed. Kelvin Knight (Notre Dame, IN: University of Notre Dame Press, 1998), p.271.
55. This point is made by Porter, 'Tradition in the Recent Work of Alasdair MacIntyre', p.44. For an example, see MacIntyre, *After Virtue*, pp.xiv-xv.
56. See Talal Asad, *Formations of the Secular: Christianity, Islam, Modernity* (Stanford, CA: Stanford University Press, 2003); Charles Taylor, *A Secular Age* (Cambridge, MA: Harvard University Press, 2007).
57. Kelvin Knight, 'After Tradition?: Heidegger *or* MacIntyre, Aristotle *and* Marx', *Analyse & Kritik* 30 (2008), p.48.
58. MacIntyre, *Whose Justice? Which Rationality?*, p.336.
59. MacIntyre, *Whose Justice? Which Rationality?*, p.340.
60. MacIntyre, *Whose Justice? Which Rationality?*, p.337. See also John Christman, *Social and Political Philosophy: A Contemporary Introduction* (London and New York: Routledge, 2002), pp.95-96.
61. MacIntyre, *Whose Justice? Which Rationality?*, pp.334-35. See MacIntyre, *After Virtue*, pp.6-8.
62. MacIntyre, *Whose Justice? Which Rationality?*, pp.342-43. Both MacIntyre and Charles Taylor mention Descartes as a key figure in the shift to the conception of a subject floating free of tradition. MacIntyre, *The Tasks of Philosophy*, pp.8-9; Charles Taylor, *Sources of the Self: The Making of the Modern Identity* (Cambridge: Cambridge University Press, 1989), pp.156-57.
63. MacIntyre, *Whose Justice? Which Rationality?*, pp.343-44. See also MacIntyre, *After Virtue*, p.250.
64. MacIntyre, *Whose Justice? Which Rationality?*, pp.336, 344.
65. MacIntyre, *Whose Justice? Which Rationality?*, p.344. A similar statement could be applied to the Sunnite Islamic tradition as it developed in history. The Māturīdite perspective developed below potentially challenges this by embedding a consistent idea of wisdom at the core of questions of justice.

66. MacIntyre, *Whose Justice? Which Rationality?*, p.344.
67. A significant strand of the Māturīdite tradition concurs on the rejection of inspiration as binding within the social order. For instance, the Ḥanafite-Māturīdite jurist ʿAlā' al-Dīn al-Samarqandī (d. 539/1144) states that a non-prophet's inspired convictions about the Law are personally binding but are not to be applied to other people. ʿAlā' al-Dīn al-Samarqandī, *Mīzān al-uṣūl fī natā'ij al-ʿuqūl*, ed. ʿAbd al-Malik ʿAbd al-Raḥmān al-Saʿdī (Makkah: Jāmiʿa Umm al-Qurā, 1984), vol.2, p.1027. Cf. Abū Manṣūr al-Māturīdī, *Kitāb al-tawḥīd*, ed. Bekir Topaloğlu and Muḥammad Aruçi, 2nd edn (Istanbul: Maktabat al-Irshād, 2010), p.69.
68. McKenny, 'Moral Disagreement and the Limits of Reason', p.212.
69. This can potentially manifest in a form of secularism in which religion is separated from the state, though this does not necessarily have to be the case. A contemporary example is the similar liberal morality that characterizes both the UK and the USA, despite the former's established Church and, in the words of Jefferson, the latter's "wall of separation between Church & State." Thomas Jefferson, 'Letter to the Danbury Baptists', *Library of Congress Information Bulletin* 57(6) (1998).
70. John Rawls, 'The Idea of an Overlapping Consensus', *Oxford Journal of Legal Studies* 7(1) (1987), pp.4-5.
71. Fadel, 'The True, the Good and the Reasonable', pp.4-5.
72. Fadel, 'The True, the Good and the Reasonable', p.5.
73. For an extended survey of such theories, see Majid Khadduri, *The Islamic Conception of Justice* (London and Baltimore: Johns Hopkins University Press, 1984).
74. See Jackson, *On the Boundaries of Theological Tolerance in Islam*, pp.16-29.
75. See the discussion in Harvey, *The Qur'an and the Just Society*, pp.27-38. Jackson devotes a single chapter to each of these schools of thought and one to Traditionalism, which amounts to an analysis of the influential recasting of the Traditionalist stance by the relatively late figure of Ibn Taymiyyah (d. 728/1328). Jackson, *Islam and the Problem of Black Suffering*.
76. Harvey, *The Qur'an and the Just Society*, pp.41-42.
77. Ulrich Rudolph, *Al-Māturīdī and the Development of Sunnī Theology in Samarqand*, trans. Rodrigo Adem (Leiden: Brill, 2015), pp.321-22. The extent to which aspects of al-Māturīdī's theology are already present in the thought of Abū Ḥanīfah depends in part on the authenticity of various treatises ascribed to the earlier figure, which I cannot discuss here. But it is impossible to claim that al-Māturīdī was merely practicing Abū Ḥanīfah's theology without ignoring the theological developments in the two intervening centuries from which al-Māturīdī draws considerably in constructing his system.
78. For many examples of theological reformulation within the Māturīdite tradition, see Harvey, *Transcendent God, Rational World*.
79. Jackson, *On the Boundaries of Theological Tolerance in Islam*, pp.8-9; Gordon D. Kaufman, *The Theological Imagination: Constructing the Concept of God* (Philadelphia, PA: The Westminster Press, 1981), pp.21-23.
80. Rotraud Wielandt, 'Main Trends of Islamic Theological Thought from the Late Nineteenth Century to Present Times', in *The Oxford Handbook of Islamic Theology*, ed. Sabine Schmidtke (Oxford: Oxford University Press, 2016), pp.749-53.
81. See MacIntyre's justification for his use of the term "NeoAristotelian" to describe his mature position. Alasdair MacIntyre, *Ethics in the Conflicts of Modernity: An Essay on Desire, Practical Reasoning, and Narrative* (Cambridge: Cambridge University Press, 2016), p.31.

82. See Thomas Hildebrandt, *Neo-Muʿtazilismus?: Intention und Kontext im modernen arabischen Umgang mit dem rationalistischen Erbe des Islam* (Leiden: Brill, 2007), pp.1-2. This often seems more of a rhetorical affiliation based on their perceived rationality and heterodoxy than genuine continuity with the theology of the classical Muʿtazilite schools.

83. Al-Māturīdī, *Kitāb al-tawḥīd*, p.164. See Harvey, *The Qur'an and the Just Society*, p.29.

84. Al-Māturīdī, *Kitāb al-tawḥīd*, p.163.

85. J. Meric Pessagno, 'The Uses of Evil in Maturidian Thought', *Studia Islamica* 60 (1984), p.63; Rudolph, *Al-Māturīdī and the Development of Sunnī Theology in Samarqand*, p.296-300; Harvey, *The Qur'an and the Just Society*, pp.28-29. See Harvey, *Transcendent God, Rational World*, pp.161-64.

86. Harvey, *The Qur'an and the Just Society*, pp.35-38. There are certainly points of similarity between the theological ethics of al-Māturīdī and that of Ibn Taymiyyah many centuries later, though there is not space to explore them here. See Sophia Vasalou, *Ibn Taymiyya's Theological Ethics* (Oxford: Oxford University Press, 2016), p.142; Jon Hoover, *Ibn Taymiyya's Theodicy of Perpetual Optimism* (Leiden: Brill, 2007), p.220.

87. Al-Māturīdī, *Kitāb al-tawḥīd*, p.167. Rudolph, *Al-Māturīdī and the Development of Sunnī Theology in Samarqand*, pp.263-64.

88. Al-Māturīdī, *Kitāb al-tawḥīd*, p.168.

89. That human beings are always obligated to act in basic matters of rationally appreciable morality is found in al-Māturīdī, *Kitāb al-tawḥīd*, pp.176 and 249. It is a mainstay of the Samarqandī and Iraqī Ḥanafite traditions, and the Muʿtazilites. The Bukhāran Ḥanafites were closer to the Ashʿarites in suspending obligation until the arrival of revelation. See A. Kevin Reinhart, *Before Revelation: The Boundaries of Muslim Moral Thought* (Albany: The State University of New York Press, 1995), pp.44-56.

90. Harvey, *The Qur'an and the Just Society*, p.37.

91. Abū al-Muʿīn al-Nasafī, *Bahr al-kalām*, ed. Walī al-Dīn Muḥammad Ṣāliḥ al-Farfūr (Damascus: Dār al-Farfūr, 2000), pp.291-92; Al-Samarqandī, *Mīzān al-uṣūl fī natā'ij al-ʿuqūl*, vol.2, p.1059; Abū Manṣūr al-Māturīdī, *Ta'wīlāt al-qur'ān*, eds Ertuğrul Boynukalin, and Bekir Topaloğlu (Istanbul: Dār al-Mīzān, 2006), vol.1, p.257. See Ramon Harvey, 'Al-Māturīdī on the Abrogation of the *Sharīʿa* in the Qur'an and Previous Scriptures', in *İmâm Mâtürîdî ve Te'vîlâtü'l-Kur'ân*, eds. Hatice K. Arpaguş, Mehmet Ümit and Bilal Kır (Istanbul: M. Ü. İlâhiyat Fakültesi Vakfi Yayınları, 2019), pp.514-17.

92. Al-Nasafī, *Bahr al-kalām*, p.292.

93. Harvey, *The Qur'an and the Just Society*, p.41.

94. Al-Māturīdī, *Ta'wīlāt al-qur'ān*, vol.6, p.392; vol.15, p.125. See Harvey, *The Qur'an and the Just Society*, p.41. Note that I treat the terms *ʿillah* (legal cause), *ḥikmah* and *maʿnā* (ontological cause) as synonymous in this context. Also see Harvey, 'Al-Māturīdī on the Abrogation of the *Sharīʿa* in the Qur'an and Previous Scriptures', pp.521-22.

95. Harvey, *The Qur'an and the Just Society*, p.58.

96. The dominant position in the classical Ḥanafite tradition is that neither *qiyās* (analogy), the main acknowledged rational method in legal theory, nor *ijmāʿ*, which can be treated in some sense as an aggregation of the *ijtihād* of ulema, provides acceptable evidence for abrogating Qur'anic rulings, due to their non-occurrence in the Prophet Muḥammad's lifetime. Fakhr al-Islām al-Bazdawī, *Uṣūl al-Bazdawī*, ed. Sā'id Bakdāsh (Madinah: Dār al-Sirāj; Beirut: Dār al-Bashā'ir al-Islāmiyyah, 2014), p.495. But some classical scholars from the Shāfiʿite school did accept abrogation of the Qur'an by types of *qiyās*, whereas even

some Ḥanafites accepted it for *ijmāᶜ*. ᶜAbd al-ᶜAzīz al-Bukhārī, *Kashf al-asrār ᶜan uṣūl Fakhr al-Islām al-Bazdawī*, ed. Aḥmad Khalūṣī and Muṣṭafā Darwīsh (Durr Saᶜādah, 1891), vol.3, pp.174-76.

97. See Harvey, *The Qur'an and the Just Society*, p.22.

98. Al-Māturīdī, *Kitāb al-tawḥīd*, pp.166, 175, 248. See Pessagno, 'The Uses of Evil in Maturidian Thought', p.76.

99. I am grateful to Hisham Altalib for pointing out the relevance of the verse for this part of my argument.

100. See MacIntyre, *Dependent Rational Animals*, p.93.

101. See Ebrahim Moosa, 'Ethical Landscape: Laws, Norms, and Morality', in *Islam in the Modern World*, ed. Jeffrey T. Kenney and Ebrahim Moosa (Abingdon: Routledge, 2014), pp.39-40.

102. See Harvey, *The Qur'an and the Just Society*, pp.41-42.

103. David Miller, 'Justice', in *The Stanford Encyclopedia of Philosophy* (Fall 2017 Edition), ed. Edward N. Zalta, (https://plato.stanford.edu/archives/fall2017/entries/justice/).

104. Jackson, *Islam and the Problem of Black Suffering*, p.103.

105. MacIntyre, *After Virtue*, p.252.

106. Cf. Al-Samarqandī, *Mīzān al-uṣūl fī natā'ij al-ᶜuqūl*, vol.1, pp.271-74.

Bibliography

Anjum, Ovamir, 'Islam as a Discursive Tradition: Talal Asad and His Interlocutors', *Comparative Studies of South Asia, Africa and the Middle East* 27(3) (2007), pp.656-72.

Aristotle, *The Politics*, trans. Carnes Lord. Chicago, IL: University of Chicago Press, 1984.

Asad, Talal. *Formations of the Secular: Christianity, Islam, Modernity*. Stanford, CA: Stanford University Press, 2003.

al-Bazdawī, Fakhr al-Islām. *Uṣūl al-Bazdawī*, ed. Sā'id Bakdāsh. Madinah: Dār al-Sirāj; Beirut: Dār al-Bashā'ir al-Islāmiyyah, 2014.

Brodersen, Angelika. 'New Light on the Emergence of Māturīdism: Abū Shakūr al-Sālimī (Fifth/Eleventh Century) and his *Kitāb al-tamhīd fī bayan al-tawḥīd*', *Journal of Islamic Studies*, 31(3) (2020), pp.329-57.

al-Bukhārī, ᶜAbd al-ᶜAzīz, *Kashf al-asrār ᶜan uṣūl Fakhr al-Islām al-Bazdawī*, ed. Aḥmad Khalūṣī and Muṣṭafā Darwīsh, 4 vols. Durr Saᶜādah, 1891.

Christman, John, *Social and Political Philosophy: A Contemporary Introduction*. London and New York: Routledge, 2002.

Dorroll, Philip, 'Modern by Tradition: Abū Manṣūr al-Māturīdī and the New Turkish Theology', PhD dissertation. Emory University, 2013.

Fadel, Mohammad, 'The True, the Good and the Reasonable: The Theological and Ethical Roots of Public Reason in Islamic Law', *Canadian Journal of Law and Jurisprudence* 21(1) (2008), pp.1-65.

Gadamer, Hans-Georg, *Truth and Method*. London and New York: Bloomsbury, 2013.

Hallaq, Wael B., *Restating Orientalism: A Critique of Modern Knowledge*. New York: Columbia University Press, 2018.

Harvey, Ramon, *The Qur'an and the Just Society*. Edinburgh: Edinburgh University Press, 2018.

___ 'Al-Māturīdī on the Abrogation of the *Sharīʿa* in the Qur'an and Previous Scriptures', in *İmâm Mâtürîdî ve Te'vîlâtü'l-Kur'ân*, eds. Hatice K. Arpaguş, Mehmet Ümit and Bilal Kır. Istanbul: M. Ü. İlâhiyat Fakültesi Vakfı Yayınları, 2019, pp.511-24.

___, *Transcendent God, Rational World: A Māturīdī Theology*. Edinburgh: Edinburgh University Press, 2021.

Herdt, Jennifer A., 'Alasdair MacIntyre's "Rationality of Traditions" and Tradition-Transcendental Standards of Justification', *The Journal of Religion* 78(4) (October 1998), pp.524-46.

Hildebrandt, Thomas, *Neo-Muʿtazilismus?: Intention und Kontext im modernen arabischen Umgang mit dem rationalistischen Erbe des Islam*. Leiden: Brill, 2007.

Hoover, Jon, *Ibn Taymiyya's Theodicy of Perpetual Optimism*. Leiden: Brill, 2007.

Jackson, Sherman, *On the Boundaries of Theological Tolerance in Islam: Abū Ḥāmid al-Ghāzalī's* Fayṣal al-Tafriqa Bayna al-Islām wa al-Zandaqa. Oxford: Oxford University Press, 2002.

___, *Islam and the Problem of Black Suffering*. Oxford: Oxford University Press, 2009.

___, 'Not Truth But Tolerance: A (Much Belated) Response to Atif Khalil', *American Journal of Islamic Social Sciences (AJISS)* 28(4) (2011), pp.146-61.

Jefferson, Thomas, 'Letter to the Danbury Baptists', *Library of Congress Information Bulletin* 57(6) (1998).

Kaufman, Gordon D., *The Theological Imagination: Constructing the Concept of God*. Philadelphia, PA: The Westminster Press, 1981.

Khadduri, Majid, *The Islamic Conception of Justice*. London and Baltimore: Johns Hopkins University Press, 1984.

Knight, Kelvin, 'After Tradition?: Heidegger *or* MacIntyre, Aristotle *and* Marx', *Analyse & Kritik* 30 (2008), pp.33-52.

MacIntyre, Alasdair, *Whose Justice? Which Rationality?* London: Duckworth, 1988.

___, *Three Rival Versions of Moral Enquiry: Encyclopaedia, Genealogy, and Tradition: Being Gifford Lectures Delivered in the University of Edinburgh in 1988*. London: Duckworth, 1990.

___, 'A Partial Response to My Critics', in *After MacIntyre: Critical Perspectives on the Work of Alasdair MacIntyre*, eds. John Horton and Susan Mendes. Notre Dame, IN: University of Notre Dame Press, 1994, pp.283-304.

___, 'An Interview for *Cogito*', in *The MacIntyre Reader*, ed. Kelvin Knight. Notre Dame, IN: University of Notre Dame Press, 1998, pp.267-75.

___, 'First Principles, Final Ends, and Contemporary Philosophical Issues', in *The MacIntyre Reader*, ed. Kelvin Knight. Notre Dame, IN: University of Notre Dame Press, 1998, pp.171-201.

___, 'Moral Relativism, Truth and Justification', in *The MacIntyre Reader*, ed. Kelvin Knight. Notre Dame, IN: University of Notre Dame Press, 1998, pp.202-20.

___, 'Practical Rationalities as Forms of Social Structure', in *The MacIntyre Reader*, ed. Kelvin Knight. Notre Dame, IN: University of Notre Dame Press, 1998, pp.120-35.

___, *Dependent Rational Animals: Why Human Beings Need the Virtues*. Chicago: Carus, 1999.

___, *The Tasks of Philosophy: Selected Essays, Volume 1*. Cambridge: Cambridge University Press, 2006.

___, *After Virtue: A Study in Moral Theory*, 3rd edn. Notre Dame, IN: University of Notre Dame Press, 2007.

___, 'Intractable Moral Disagreements', in *Intractable Disputes about the Natural Law*, ed.

Lawrence S. Cunningham. Notre Dame, IN: University of Notre Dame Press, 2009, pp.1-52.
—, *Ethics in the Conflicts of Modernity: An Essay on Desire, Practical Reasoning, and Narrative*. Cambridge: Cambridge University Press, 2016.
al-Māturīdī, Abū Manṣūr, *Ta'wīlāt al-qur'ān*, eds Ertuğrul Boynukalin, and Bekir Topaloğlu, 18 vols. Istanbul: Dār al-Mīzān, 2006.
—, *Kitāb al-tawḥīd*, ed. Bekir Topaloğlu and Muḥammad Aruçi, 2nd edn. Istanbul: Maktabat al-Irshād, 2010.
McKenny, Gerald, 'Moral Disagreement and the Limits of Reason: Reflections on MacIntyre and Ratzinger', in *Intractable Disputes about the Natural Law*, ed. Lawrence S. Cunningham. Notre Dame, IN: University of Notre Dame Press, 2009, pp.195-226.
McMylor, Peter, 'Marxism and Christianity: Dependencies and Differences in Alasdair MacIntyre's Critical Social Thought', *Theoria* 55(116) (2008), pp.45-66.
Miller, David, 'Justice', in *The Stanford Encyclopedia of Philosophy* (Fall 2017 Edition), ed. Edward N. Zalta, (https://plato.stanford.edu/archives/fall2017/entries/justice/).
Moosa, Ebrahim, 'Ethical Landscape: Laws, Norms, and Morality', in *Islam in the Modern World*, ed. Jeffrey T. Kenney and Ebrahim Moosa. Abingdon: Routledge, 2014, pp.35-55.
al-Nasafī, Abū al-Muʿīn, *Bahr al-kalām*, ed. Walī al-Dīn Muḥammad Ṣāliḥ al-Farfūr. Damascus: Dār al-Farfūr, 2000.
Pangle, Thomas L., and Timothy W. Burns, *The Key Texts of Political Philosophy: An Introduction*. Cambridge: Cambridge University Press, 2014.
Pessagno, J. Meric, 'The Uses of Evil in Maturidian Thought', *Studia Islamica* 60 (1984), pp.59-82.
Porter, Jean, 'Tradition in the Recent Work of Alasdair MacIntyre', in *Alasdair MacIntyre*, ed. Mark C. Murphy. Cambridge: Cambridge University Press, 2003, pp.38-69.
Rahman, Fazlur, *Revival and Reform in Islam: A Study of Islamic Fundamentalism*. Oxford: Oneworld, 2000.
Rawls, John, 'The Idea of an Overlapping Consensus', *Oxford Journal of Legal Studies* 7(1) (1987), pp.1-25.
Reinhart, A. Kevin, *Before Revelation: The Boundaries of Muslim Moral Thought*. Albany: The State University of New York Press, 1995.
Rudolph, Ulrich, *Al-Māturīdī and the Development of Sunnī Theology in Samarqand*, trans. Rodrigo Adem. Leiden: Brill, 2015.
al-Samarqandī, ʿAlā' al-Dīn, *Mīzān al-uṣūl fī natā'ij al-ʿuqūl*, ed. ʿAbd al-Malik ʿAbd al-Raḥmān al-Saʿdī, 2 vols. Makkah: Jāmiʿah Umm al-Qurā, 1984.
Schmidtke, Sabine, 'Introduction', in *The Oxford Handbook of Islamic Theology*, ed. Sabine Schmidtke. Oxford: Oxford University Press, 2016.
Taylor, Charles, *Sources of the Self: The Making of the Modern Identity*. Cambridge: Cambridge University Press, 1989.
—, *A Secular Age*. Cambridge, MA: Harvard University Press, 2007.
Trenery, David, *Alasdair MacIntyre, George Lindbeck, and the Nature of Tradition*. Eugene, OR: Wipf and Stock Publishers, 2014.
Vasalou, Sophia, *Ibn Taymiyya's Theological Ethics*. Oxford: Oxford University Press, 2016.
Wielandt, Rotraud, 'Main Trends of Islamic Theological Thought from the Late Nineteenth Century to Present Times', in *The Oxford Handbook of Islamic Theology*, ed. Sabine Schmidtke. Oxford: Oxford University Press, 2016, pp.707-64.

PART 2

REGIONAL DISCOURSES OF FEMINISM AND HERMENEUTICS

3

The Hermeneutics of Justice: Hidayet Şefkatli Tuksal and the Artistry of the Qur'an

Philip Dorroll

Introduction

This chapter explores the unique and compelling theory of Qur'anic hermeneutics proposed by the Turkish theologian Hidayet Şefkatli Tuksal. Tuksal's work shows that the encounter between the human and the divine in the process of revelation forms the hermeneutical basis of divine and human justice. Because the process of revelation necessitates contact between the eternal and the contingent, the divine and the human, Tuksal employs a particularly evocative metaphor for this encounter: she analogizes the Qur'anic text with an artistic product, describing how contingent historical material is "woven" into the "fabric" of the revelation.

Yet she distinguishes between this functional structure of the revelation and the eternal content of the divine message, which can only be apprehended by viewing the "work" of the Qur'an as a whole. This whole is composed of the interconnectedness of strands of the historical and eternal woven together in a single text that presents a coherent and universally applicable message of justice and human dignity in the service of the one God. As well as analysing Tuksal's hermeneutical theory, this chapter will discuss how she applies it to one of the most difficult verses in the Qur'an, 4:34.

Hidayet Şefkatli Tuksal (b. 1963 in Ankara) is one of the most prominent public voices at the intersection of academic theology and social justice activism in contemporary Turkey. A native of the Turkish capital and a pious Muslim, Tuksal received her PhD from Ankara University in 1998. Two years later, her first book was published, *Kadın Karşıtı Söylemin İslam*

Geleneğindeki İzdüşümleri (*Projections of Misogynistic Discourse in Islamic Tradition*).[1] Her dissertation and book (the latter of which will form the basis of my analysis of her Qur'anic hermeneutics below) are groundbreaking theological analyses in modern Turkish, possibly the first examples of systematic feminist Islamic theology written in the Turkish Republic.

In addition to her path-breaking academic work, Tuksal has been a prominent voice for the advancement of human rights and civil society in Turkey for over two decades.[2] Her activism has focused on issues of individual freedom of expression and autonomy, most especially the legal rights and social treatment of headscarf-wearing women under Turkish secularism.[3] Her vocal advocacy of the right of women to self-expression through wearing the headscarf reflects her support for other issues related to individual rights, bodily autonomy, and justice.

For instance, she has publicly opposed calls to legally ban abortion (despite her personal opposition to the procedure in some cases) and has severely criticized the ways the Turkish government has attempted to politically instrumentalize an issue that she argues has very complex personal, social, and medical implications.[4] She has also criticized general homophobia[5] and prevailing norms of hegemonic masculinity in contemporary Turkey,[6] in addition to publicly exposing an incident of sexual harassment and its apparent subsequent cover-up at a Turkish high school.[7] At the time of writing, her most recent public stances on issues of individual and social justice included criticism of the suspension of rights and judicial processes under the recently lifted state of emergency,[8] and criticism of Turkish prejudice against Syrian refugees in the country.[9] She has written for a number of online media platforms in addition to being very active on Twitter, where she has a large following particularly among Turkish public intellectuals and members of the current political opposition, and formerly taught at Mardin Artuklu University. She is currently a faculty member in the department of Islamic Sciences at Kırıkkale University.

General Methodology and Goals of *Projections of Misogynistic Discourse*

The central thesis of *Projections of Misogynistic Discourse* is that certain misogynistic discourses reflective of the social values of medieval Islamic societies have been codified into the Hadith tradition. In this form, these discourses have constituted the ideological backbone of existing misogynist ideologies and social practices in Muslim societies ever since. Her book is a systematic analysis of various examples of misogynistic discourses in the Hadith (and also in the Qur'an) that attempts to distinguish genuine prophetic guidance in extant Hadith literature from traces of patriarchal discourses and social practices that reflect historically contingent social environments.[10] In the course of this analysis, she uses the Qur'an as the source of basic Islamic theological and ethical principles and as a reliable guide to social practices at the time of the revelation.[11] Though her book focuses primarily on Hadith literature, the analysis below will focus on the Qur'anic hermeneutics that she systematically develops to undergird her larger critique and analysis of the Islamic religious tradition.

Tuksal's book builds on specific historiographical and theological insights that are worth briefly analyzing here, as they provide insight into the foundations of her Qur'anic hermeneutics. She first of all cites as a formative inspiration her lived experience of Muslim faith and activism, identifying the Prophet's wife ʿĀ'ishah as an example of the critical and independent spirit within the Islamic intellectual tradition that animates her own work.[12] She bases her sociological and historical analyses of patriarchy (*ataerkillik*) and the patriarchal social system (*ataerkil sistem*) on the work of numerous Turkish and non-Turkish historians of gender relations, such as Elisabeth Badinter, Gerda Lerner, and Fatmagül Berktay. For instance, Tuksal adopts Lerner's critique of the use of religious discourse to structure and support patriarchal social institutions, arguing that this is how misogynistic discourses in the Islamic tradition, particularly the Hadith, have often been used in Muslim history.[13] Tuksal also adopts Berktay's critique of the monotheistic faiths' absorption of the patriarchal social values of the societies into which they were born.[14]

Tuksal's historiographical method emphasizes the role of human agency in the historical formation of religious discourses, including the inherent subjectivity of any historical analysis of these discourses. Her methodology takes seriously the subjectivity of both the custodians and developers of Islamic religious discourses (i.e. the traditional ulema), and those who research the history and formation of these discourses. She argues that "the subjective relationship between the historian and historical material" is not an incidental but rather a determinative feature of both modern and traditional Hadith scholarship.[15] She quotes the French historian Henri Iréné Marrou in this context: "history is a spiritual adventure in which the historian's personality becomes entirely involved."[16]

Interestingly, she notes that one of the weaknesses of traditional Hadith scholarship (such as *ʿilm al-rijāl*, or *rical tenkidi*) is precisely that it alienates the researcher from her own subjectivity by forcing her to focus on the personal circumstances of the transmitters, rather than on one's self. She argues that analysis of the text of Hadith, by contrast, has the opposite effect, and she chooses this method for her own research.[17] Tuksal's work begins by taking seriously the mutually transformative effects of the encounter between the human individual and historical tradition, and as we shall see below, she expands this analysis to a theological consideration of the encounter between the human individual and divine revelation that takes place within human history.

Finally, Tuksal acknowledges her debt to the work of Fazlur Rahman, whom she mentions by name as a key influence in her own systematic theological thinking. In particular, she cites his distinction between the eternal truths of Islam and the contingent and historically variable human interpretations of, and additions to, these eternal truths.[18] Unlike her use of the scholars mentioned above, she does not cite a particular work of Rahman in this context. However, it seems likely that she is referring to Rahman's theory of "twofold movement" in Qur'anic hermeneutics that "move[s] from the concrete case treatments of the Qur'an—taking the necessary and relevant social conditions of that time into account—to the general principles upon which the entire teaching converges" and then forward toward new considerations of Islamic practices and legislation based on this historically contextualized analysis.[19]

It is worth noting that Tuksal's use of Rahman's work connects her with the broader global phenomenon of Islamic feminist and Muslimah theology that has flourished in the past few decades. Safet Bektovic has pointed out that the exploration of "the relationship between the normative and the historical" forms the core of Rahman's theology.[20] Rahman's formulation of the common Islamic modernist distinction between the eternal truths of religion and their historically contingent (and therefore changeable) expression plays a major role in her theological system. As Aysha A. Hidayatullah notes, this distinction has played a key role in other systematic feminist and Muslimah theologies in the 20th and 21st centuries, particularly due to Rahman's widely influential formulation of this distinction as "a model for distinguishing the Qur'an's universal moral values from its more specific pronouncements aimed at its immediate seventh-century audience of revelation."[21] As will be demonstrated below, Tuksal develops these insights in an original way by elaborating on the specific theological consequences of the encounter between the human and the divine in the process of revelation.

Qur'anic Hermeneutics

Tuksal's Qur'anic hermeneutics are based on certain key distinctions she makes within the nature and structure of the Qur'an itself. She argues that the Qur'an possesses a "transcendent" (*aşkın*) essence while also exhibiting a "functional structure" (*işlevsel yapı*).[22] In other words, built into the Qur'an is the fundamental theological distinction between the divine and the human, the eternal and the contingent. She elaborates on this distinction this way:

> In its function (*işlev*) as the sending down, through human means, of the transcendent truths that constitute the general characteristic of divine revelation; thereby weaving as a backdrop (*fon*) the phenomena, problems, general assumptions, traditions, and beliefs of the environment in which it was revealed – in short, the world of its first addressees – on a number of topics of interest to human kind, [the Qur'an] consists of representative rulings and solutions, recommendations, and principles (*prensipler*) that carry the possibility of wider development.[23]

This dense and evocative passage reveals the most important details of Tuksal's Qur'anic hermeneutics. The artistic metaphors that she uses, such as the concepts of "weaving" and "backdrop," are the most intriguing components of her hermeneutical theory, and therefore require sustained elaboration in order to clarify exactly what she means when distinguishing between the transcendent and functional dimensions of the Qur'anic text.

First of all, the passage above implies a basic distinction between the eternal message of the text (the content of which will be elaborated shortly) and the historical environment into which this message is inserted. Tuksal's theory is particularly sensitive to the fact that revelation itself implies an absolute distinction between the message and the recipient, the necessary eternality of God's capacity to communicate and the contingency of the human addressee. Rather than simply posit this distinction, Tuksal's theology delves deeply into its implications for scriptural hermeneutics.

Given this necessary distinction, how can the contact that occurs in the revelatory process between the divine and the human be conceptualized?

If they are absolutely ontologically distinct, can we conceptualize their contact at all? Tuksal here proposes the metaphor of weaving: strands of the eternal content of the divine message and the cultural environment into which it was revealed are woven together in the single Qur'anic text. This metaphor expresses both the distance and the closeness between the divine and the human, the eternal and the contingent, within the revelatory process. It expresses their distance because within a piece of woven fabric, no matter how tightly the different strands are woven together, the strands remain ontologically distinct – they cannot melt or merge into each other. At the same time, these strands may be so tightly woven together that the distinction between them may be very hard for the observer to detect. Moreover, the relationship between the strands within a piece of woven fabric is what constitutes the fabric itself – they cannot be extricated from each other without destroying the composition as a whole.

A particularly evocative dimension of this artistic metaphor is Tuksal's use of the term *fon*. This is a very specific term that when used to mean "backdrop" has connotations particular to fine arts: it can be used to refer specifically to the backdrop of a theater set, the underlying layer of a painting, or of a woven piece of fabric. "Backdrop" here suggests a layer of an artistic work that, though hidden or less prominent, nevertheless serves as foundational for the way the work presents itself to the viewer (or reader). In other words, as "backdrop" the cultural context of the revelation cannot simply be brushed aside: it forms the necessary foundation of the total masterpiece of God's revelation. Yet at the same time, the backdrop is not itself the primary content or message of this revelation, which can only be apprehended by viewing the work as a whole.

Finally, the passage suggests the idea of hermeneutical development while at the same time pointing out that not all injunctions in the Qur'anic text have the same theological or ethical status. Some of the injunctions that emerge from the totality of the Qur'anic work are "representative"[24] or "recommendations" that are presumably not meant to be implemented in all times and places. On the other hand, the totality of the Qur'anic work also presents certain "principles" the nature of which is to continue their development forward in time beyond the revelation. As will be explained, these principles form the eternal content of the divine message and it is their implementation and conscious cultivation on both an individual and social level in differing cultural and historical contexts that forms the core of Islamic ethics.

Tuksal further elaborates on this artistic metaphor in a second crucial passage:

> When viewing the issue from the perspective of the divine, when these manifestations [of the central content of the Qur'anic message] that carry very clear and certain outlines are sent down to the human plane, in the particularity of every human individual and with the entirety of the conditions and specificities that are shared with or separate from other human beings, [these manifestations] transform into a cluster of images and conditions, as if undergoing a mathematical permutation. A portion of these images, as reflections of the social realities and conditions connected with the first generation to be addressed by the divine message, are woven tightly into the fabric (*doku*)[25] of the Qur'an.[26]

Here Tuksal describes in further detail precisely what happens when the eternal content of the divine message interacts with the contingent circumstances of the historical environment in which it was revealed. The eternal truths of the Qur'anic message, in order to be instantiated within human circumstances, emerge from this encounter as a "cluster of images and conditions" that are "woven tightly into the fabric" of the text as a whole. The process of revelation necessitates the "permutation" of eternal truths into forms that can be readily comprehended by human audiences, but these forms are necessarily historically contingent and thus must be analyzed as such when interpreting the divine message of the Qur'anic text. As we will see later, some of these forms are, in fact, the traces of patriarchal social tradition that her book aims to identify and analyze.

In sum, Tuksal's theory of Qur'anic hermeneutics is based on a consideration of the theological implications of the meeting of the eternal and the contingent, the divine and the human, in the process of revelation. This focus allows Tuksal to develop a sophisticated artistic metaphor for how to understand the process of revelation, the process that resulted in the instantiation of the Islamic revelation in the historical world. In particular, Tuksal provides a compelling way to conceptualize the status and function of the historical context of the Qur'an: this historical context cannot be simply discarded because it is the necessary form taken by the content of the revelation. Yet at the same time, it cannot be mistaken for the content of the Qur'anic work itself: it enables the intelligible expression of the divine message but is not the content of the message itself. This particular type of theological historicism manages to avoid both excising historicity entirely from Qur'anic hermeneutics and identifying the message of the text with the historical form of its expression.

Qur'anic Theological Anthropology

Tuksal argues that the specific content of the eternal divine message of the Qur'an is a particular theological anthropology. The basis of this theological anthropology can be found in verse 95:4: "truly we have created man (*al-insān*) in the most beautiful stature (*fī aḥsani taqwīm*)."[28] According to Tuksal, this verse exemplifies the basic Qur'anic conception of human nature: that it is inherently noble and good, and that this inherent goodness has no necessary basis in the gender, social status, or other contingent circumstances of the individual human being. Human worth and dignity are based simply on humanity and the fact of its creation as good by God.

Tuksal also cites verse 33:35 in this context:

> For submitting men and submitting women, believing men and believing women, devout men and devout women, truthful men and truthful women, patient men and patient women, humble men and humble women, charitable men and charitable women, men who fast and women who fast, men who guard their private parts and women who guard [their private parts], men who remember God often and women who remember [God often], God has prepared forgiveness and a great reward.[29]

Tuksal points out that, according to these foundational Qur'anic verses, it is the "prototype of the faithful human being" that constitutes the ideal for human ethical behavior, not a particular status as male or member of a certain social group. The verse above in particular makes absolutely clear that individual virtue is not based on a gendered hierarchy but is equally available to all human beings.

Furthermore, Tuksal interprets this verse as possessing both an individual and social dimension because it describes the Qur'anic ideal of the "context of the human-to-human and the human-to-God relationship."[30] In other words, individual virtue is not simply manifest in the way one approaches God, but also in the way one approaches other human beings. Tuksal sees the equity and egalitarianism implied by the verse as equally necessary for social relationships and structures as it is for consideration of individual human morality. Equity here means social equality and justice with respect to other persons as well as equality of individual moral actions with respect to God.

Tuksal also points to verse 16:90 as another summation of the ethical ideal of the Qur'anic message as a whole: "Truly God commands justice, virtue, and giving to kinsfolk, and He forbids indecency, wrong, and rebelliousness. And He admonishes you, that haply you may remember."[31] As with 33:35, this verse implies no gendered or otherwise socially contingent distinctions between human beings in their capacity to fulfill the ethical mandates latent in their individual humanity. Furthermore, the verse implies both an individual and social dimension of ethical action: justice (*ʿadl*) and virtue (*iḥsān*). Human beings are commanded here not only to strive for individual moral virtue, but also to strive to arrange their societies to reflect the divine ideal of justice.

This Qur'anic ethical ideal represents the development of the natural goodness instilled in human nature itself by God. Indeed, the "most fundamental mission" of the Qur'an is to serve as guidance in "actualizing [human] capacity to its highest point in order to attain the status of righteousness (*salihlik*)."[32] The basic content of human excellence and virtue demanded by the Qur'an is the actualizing of human potential through belief in the one God (*iman*) and the conscious performance of righteous deeds (*salih amel*). Nowhere does this ideal imply a distinction in gender, social class, or other contingent distinctions between individual human beings. Indeed, one key feature of this message is that it conceptualizes women as active moral subjects, rather than as passive objects of social domination or prescription.[33]

In sum, the eternal divine content of the Qur'anic revelation with respect to theological anthropology features two essential truths: that human beings are all created equal in goodness and stature, and that they are all expected to develop this goodness through belief in the one God and through doing good in the world. This is part of the eternal content of the Qur'anic message that is inserted into the historical contingencies of the revelatory process, and it is the part of the message that is most applicable to questions of human relationships.

The Hermeneutics of Justice: Taqwīm vs. Qiwāmah

Tuksal uses the hermeneutic framework and theological anthropology outlined above to tackle the most difficult parts of the "cluster of images and conditions" that make up the historical texture of the Qur'anic revelation. One of the most difficult parts of the revelation from the perspective of gender justice is the verse 4:34. Tuksal uses an artistic metaphor for the process of revelation precisely to tackle these kinds of difficult verses. The application of her unique hermeneutical method to these verses in particular is one of the most original elements of her book, and it proves a compelling method for discussing the complexities of the relationship between patriarchal tradition and scriptural ideal.

After explaining how the process of revelation results in the "backdrop" of a historical and contingent "cluster of images and conditions" that are "woven" into the very "fabric" of Qur'anic discourse, Tuksal argues that the patriarchal discourses found *within the Qur'an itself* are examples of these contingent "permutations" of the revelatory process.[34] She goes so far as to argue that patriarchal discourses in the Qur'an, and the historical customs that lay behind them, are in fact "a determinative factor in the fabric (*doku*) of the verses."[35] These contingent social conditions constitute the necessary precondition for the intelligibility of the revelation to its human audience.

Indeed, according to Tuksal, patriarchal discourse and social codes are therefore an "inevitable" feature of the divine revelation.[36] This is emphatically not because these codes are part of the eternal divine message of the text; instead, they are part of the woven backdrop of the fabric of the Qur'an as a total work and are therefore *functionally* necessary but not *morally* or *theologically* necessary. She goes on to explain how this insight into the function of patriarchal verses in the Qur'an results in a particular hermeneutic method:

> Therefore, better comprehension of the mission of divine revelation as it relates to the status of women (revelation itself being inevitably predicated upon local patriarchal codes), is nevertheless dependent on being able to analyze these codes, starting from the openings within the fissures of the [patriarchal] mentality.[37]

Identifying patriarchal discourse in the Qur'an, and in Islamic tradition more generally (as her book aims to do), is an essential part of her hermeneutics of Qur'anic justice. These structural or functional features of the text are a necessary part of its underlying composition; they are inevitable features of its "expressibility" to human addressees. Yet they are not the content of the message itself, which is contained in the theological anthropology of equity and justice outlined above. Furthermore, the "fissures," or the contradictions and conceptual weaknesses, contained within patriarchal discourse form the starting point for the analysis and ultimate critique of patriarchy within Islamic tradition.

Finally, Tuksal makes it explicit that she applies this hermeneutical framework to the analysis of the most difficult Qur'anic verses, such as 4:34. She argues that this verse, in particular, is a clear example of the contingent patriarchal codes in place at the time of the revelation. It represents in particular the economic and social dependence of women on men and their correspondingly lower place in the social hierarchy.[38] The concept of *qiwāmah* (*kavvamlık*), men's guardianship over women, is therefore a clear example of contingent and descriptive social relations; simply put, the content of this verse is not meant to apply to human beings universally. Instead, it is the theological anthropology of *taqwīm* outlined above that constitute the essential core of the Qur'anic message on gender relations. *Qiwāmah* is part of the text's historical fabric and backdrop, not the eternal message of the whole.

Tuksal's argument is noteworthy in a number of respects. First of all, it is significant that she makes no attempt to interpret the words of the verse to reflect a non-patriarchal message. She frankly acknowledges that they are patriarchal and that they were intended that way. However, her theological analysis of the process of revelation indicates that their patriarchal message does not have universal import or applicability. By making theological distinctions *within the Qur'an itself* between the eternal content of the text as a whole and the historically contingent features of the text, she is able to acknowledge the clear sense of difficult verses without arguing that these particular verses are indicative of the overall content of the Qur'an's revealed message. This method neither necessitates arguing against the clear meanings of difficult verses, nor elevating these particular verses to the status of eternal divine command. Using Tuksal's Qur'anic hermeneutics, we are able to claim that patriarchal discourse in the Qur'an is functional and contingent, not prescriptive or universal.

Comparison and Evaluation

In its broad outlines, Tuksal's approach to the study of Hadith is very similar to a 2004 study by Sa'diyya Shaikh, which argues that Hadith can be read "as a religio-cultural text that provides a mirror into the dominant conceptions of gender and the category of woman within the formative period of the Muslim legacy."[39] Like Tuksal, Shaikh's critique of patriarchy and misogynistic discourses is grounded in her religious commitment to justice as "the spiritual core of Islam."[40]

Tuksal's specifically theological and hermeneutic project follows in the tradition of Islamic modernist theology, as Tuksal herself notes above. The closest comparisons to her theological arguments can be found in this tradition. As Ziba Mir-Hosseini states, 4:34 was a particularly troubling verse for modernist theology in the 19th and 20th centuries because of its potential to provide divine sanction for oppressive social systems. Indeed, as Mir-Hosseini demonstrates, this verse has formed the basis for the concept of male authority over women (*qiwāmah*) and thus has been integral to the perpetuation of patriarchal social structures in Muslim societies.[41] Yet the plain sense of the verse poses a problem for modernist interpreters given the whole of the Qur'anic message: "The Qur'an upholds justice and exhorts Muslims to stand for justice; but it does not give us a definition of justice; rather it gives direction, the path to follow towards justice which is always time and context bound."[42] Kecia Ali makes a similar point, arguing that reconsideration of the juristic tradition necessarily invokes the theological question of God's justice.[43]

Part of Tuksal's answer to this dilemma is drawn directly from the modernist tradition: a shift in emphasis on specific verses within the Qur'anic text, or put another way, a redrawing of the boundaries between what is considered of eternal and contingent historical importance. As Ayesha S. Chaudhry reveals, the premodern Islamic interpretive tradition on 4:34 unanimously held it to be a verse with universal importance and applicability: "not a single pre-colonial Muslim scholar objected to the disciplinary privilege of husbands; they instead treated this privilege as a basic marital right."[44] Chaudhry shows that the emphasis placed on this verse in the premodern period (and the neglect of other verses that command mutual affection and love in relationships) was a result of the sheer ubiquity of patriarchal social systems, or what Chaudhry terms a patriarchal "idealized cosmology."[45] In other words, the totality of the worldview of premodern societies would have made it extremely difficult, if not downright impossible, to think outside of a patriarchal framework when interpreting a sacred text.

Karen Bauer makes a similar point about premodern interpretations of 4:34, noting that common notions of authority and political power were "predicated on the idealized vision that the stronger party (the man) should treat the weaker party (the woman) within acceptable bounds of propriety."[46] The behavior deemed to fall within those bounds was much different before the advent of the now ubiquitous modern conception of equality as the ideal mode of justice. Bauer also points out that, despite the universal premodern acceptance of patriarchal authority, the relative traditionalism or progressiveness of a given text is most effectively understood with reference to the specific constraints of its genre, methodology, and social and historical context.[47]

Modern (and especially modernist) theologians, in distinct contrast to the traditional modes of interpretation discussed above, shifted emphasis to other verses in the Qur'anic text, arguing that 4:34 does not carry universal applicability and is restricted to the time period in which it was revealed.[48] Modernist theologians of the 19th and 20th centuries have frequently argued that 30:21 carries universal import and applicability for spousal relations: "And among His signs is that He created mates for you from among yourselves, that you might find rest in them, and He established affection and mercy (*raḥmah*) between you. Truly in that are signs for a people who reflect." This verse continues to exert considerable influence in contemporary Qur'anic hermeneutics: Kecia Ali suggests that it could form the basis of an Islamic sexual ethics of "meaningful consent and mutuality."[49]

Verse 30:21 is particularly powerful because it links the spousal relationship with the paramount divine attribute of Mercy or Loving Compassion, *raḥmah*, the attribute by which God is most frequently described in the Qur'an. As we have seen above, Tuksal makes a characteristically modernist theological interpretive move when she argues for the eternal import of verses such as 33:35 while arguing that 4:34's applicability is restricted to the time period in which it was revealed. Also, like Chaudhry, Tuksal recognizes the thoroughgoing patriarchal context of the premodern period and its impact on the Islamic interpretive tradition.

Tuksal's approach also bears notable similarities to the work of amina wadud. Like Tuksal, wadud recognizes the existence of social institutions and practices in Islamic tradition, even in Islamic revelation, that are simply irredeemable by modern moral standards (a dilemma common to Jewish and Christian scripture as well). wadud gives the example of slavery: it is condoned in Islamic (and Jewish and Christian) sacred texts, but the Muslim (and Jewish and Christian) communities of the modern period have collectively decided against the morality of its continued practice. As wadud brilliantly points out, slavery was abolished in Islam without having to make the Qur'an anti-slavery.[50] wadud argues for a similar collective response, a saying "no" to the dictates of 4:34, as the Muslim community has already done with respect to other premodern practices such as slavery.[51]

Like Tuksal, wadud's theology also takes seriously the restrictions placed on human access to divine truth implied by the processes of revelation. Composed as it is of human language (even though this language was spoken by God). The Qur'an is "a window to look through," not the vision of Truth itself.[52] In a passage very reminiscent of Tuksal's overall point, wadud notes that in the process of revelation the divine "self-disclosure" was "particularized within the parameters of the socio-cultural, moral, legal, and linguistic components of that context."[53]

Both Tuksal and wadud therefore emphasize the importance of human agency in the interpretive process and the establishment of justice in the world, based precisely on the divine acknowledgment of such agency in the encounter of revelation. According to wadud, the ethical paradigm implied by *tawḥīd*, the singleness of God, means that humans are empowered and made responsible by God for the establishment of justice in this world.[54] God is just and demands justice: if humans set up oppressive social structures, they are directly contradicting God's clear command and are thus responsible for the re-establishment of justice in the world.[55] Put another way, wadud and Tuksal are connected by their reorientation of Islamic theology of revelation, reminiscent of Fazlur Rahman, toward a consideration of "the ethical-moral foundation" and implications of Islamic practice and the revealed law.[56]

Yet there are important questions that remain unanswered in Tuksal's analysis. Tuksal does not argue for a reading against the grain of the plain meaning of 4:34. Hidayatullah, Chaudhry, and Tuksal all point out that the plain meaning of the text does indeed sanction violence, or at the very least what Chaudhry calls male "disciplinary privilege."[57] Tuksal, however, argues that this permission is a reflection of patriarchal social structures in place at the time of the revelation and is not meant by God to be a universal command or permission beyond the historical time period in which it was revealed (as with slavery, for instance).

Chaudhry points out, however, that this verse was apparently revealed in response to the Prophet Muhammad's refusal to strike his wives (according to extant historical material, he was well-known to have never struck his wives in any way throughout his life). The verse was revealed to provide permission for someone to do so after the Prophet explicitly counseled against it.[58] Tuksal's analysis does not explicitly take this historical context into account: what does it mean for Prophetic practice to differ from explicit divine permission here? Moreover, as Chaudhry points out, even if the verse is understood to not command violence but rather a kind of "disciplinary privilege" (an argument that even many premodern interpreters made), why would God sanction such a power imbalance between the sexes in any historical period? The Qur'an shows no hesitancy at all in challenging other social practices of the time: why did it leave some unchallenged and roundly condemn others?[59]

Hidayatullah's profound reflections on these issues raise similar dilemmas. Her analysis of the Qur'anic text reveals that there may simply be differing ethical systems at work within the text itself: some verses command hierarchy, some mutuality and egalitarianism. She suggests that these values may only seem contradictory in the eyes of modern interpreters but may not have seemed so at the time of the revelation; thus, the Qur'an cannot as a single document be said to be in complete accord with contemporary egalitarian views of social relations.[60] If this was the case during the period in which the revelation occurred, then how can modernist interpreters claim to prioritize some verses over others? Moreover, do the ethical demands of egalitarianism demand the construction of value systems that are, in at least some sense, "extra-Qur'anic"? If this is the case, how can we understand the divinity of the text if its values systems appear to be so historically malleable, differing, and particularized?[61]

Conclusion

Tuksal's work is admirable for its sophistication and its courage – it confronts difficult elements of Islamic scripture and tradition from a pious point of view that brings sophisticated theological analysis to bear on complex hermeneutical problems. As alluded to above, this problem is by no means unique to Islamic scripture. Tuksal's hermeneutical theory suggests a much wider theological utility for conceiving of sacred scripture as a work of artistry produced by the interaction between humans and the Divine.

More precisely, scripture is the artwork of the eternal painted on temporal canvasses; the vision of God refracted through human prisms. Tuksal's work raises as many questions as it answers, but the trajectory it suggests, toward a hermeneutics of the divine-human encounter that is multi-directional and multi-faceted, could lead to theological bases for justice that respect both the complexities of social nuance and the concreteness of absolute moral direction. God's justice may best be understood as a production of the interweaving of divine and human in the religious encounter: ontologically separate, yet eternally bound.

Endnotes

1. Citations from this text will be taken from the OTTO Yayınları printing, which to the best of my knowledge is the most recent (Ankara, 2014). The book was first published by Kitabiyat Yayınları (Ankara, 2000). There is no full English translation of this text; the only English version of its contents I have been able to locate is a short article-length summary of its main arguments: see Hidayet Şefkatli Tuksal, 'Misogynistic Reports in the Hadith Literature', in *Muslima Theology: The Voices of Muslim Women Theologians*, eds. Ednan Aslan, Marcia Hermansen, and Elif Medeni (Frankfurt am Main: Peter Lang, 2013), pp.133-154.
2. A very brief summary of some themes in her theological work can be found in Philip Dorroll, 'Post-Gezi Islamic Theology: Intersectional Islamic Feminism in Turkey', *Review of Middle East Studies* 50(2) (2017), pp.161-64. Her activism has been described, or touched upon, in a number of relevant studies. See Hürcan Aslı Aksoy, 'Invigorating Democracy in Turkey: The Agency of Organized Islamist Women', *Politics and Gender* 11 (2015), pp.159-66; Yeşim Arat, 'Islamist Women and Feminist Concerns in Contemporary Turkey', *Frontiers* 37(3) (2016), pp.128, 140-42; Brigitte Jelen, 'Educated, Independent, and Covered: The Professional Aspirations and Experiences of University-educated hijabi in Contemporary Turkey', *Women's Studies International Forum* 34 (2011), pp.316-17; Anna C. Korteweg and Gökçe Yurdakul, *The Headscarf Debates: Conflicts of National Belonging* (Palo Alto, CA: Stanford University Press, 2014), p.92; and Mona Tajali, 'Islamic Women's Groups and the

Quest for Political Representation in Turkey and Iran', *The Middle East Journal* 69(4) (2015), p.573.

3. See Aksoy, 'Invigorating Democracy in Turkey', p.161; Jelen, 'Educated, Independent, and Covered', pp.316-17; Korteweg and Yurdakul, *The Headscarf Debates*, p.92; and Tajali, 'Islamic Women's Groups and the Quest for Political Representation', p.573.

4. Aksoy, 'Invigorating Democracy in Turkey', p.165; Arat, 'Islamist Women and Feminist Concerns in Contemporary Turkey', p.142.

5. Aksoy, 'Invigorating Democracy in Turkey', p.163.

6. Arat, 'Islamist Women and Feminist Concerns in Contemporary Turkey', p.140; Dorroll, 'Post-Gezi Islamic Theology', p.164.

7. Arat, 'Islamist Women and Feminist Concerns in Contemporary Turkey', p.141.

8. Hidayet Şefkatli Tuksal, 'Adalet Bekliyoruz!', *Serbestiyet*, January 19, 2017; and Hidayet Şefkatli Tuksal, 'OHAL'de hukuka riayet', *Serbestiyet*, Februry 11, 2017. Both available at: http://serbestiyet.com.

9. Hidayet Şefkatli Tuksal, 'Türkler Suriyelilerle birlikte yaşamaya hazır görünmüyor', *Hürriyet*, May 10, 2018. Available at: http://www.hurriyet.com.tr/turkler-suriyelilerle-birlikte-yasamaya-hazir-40832069.

10. Hidayet Şefkatli Tuksal, *Kadın Karşıtı Söylemin İslam Geleneğindeki İzdüşümleri* (Ankara: OTTO Yayinları 2014), pp.28-33.

11. Tuksal, *Kadın Karşıtı Söylemin İslam Geleneğindeki İzdüşümleri*, p.31.

12. Tuksal, 'Misogynistic Reports in the Hadith Literature', p.133.

13. Tuksal, *Kadın Karşıtı Söylemin İslam Geleneğindeki İzdüşümleri*, p.39; on this point she cites Gerda Lerner, *The Creation of Patriarchy* (Oxford: Oxford University Press, 1986), pp.16-17.

14. Tuksal, *Kadın Karşıtı Söylemin İslam Geleneğindeki İzdüşümleri*, p.21; on this point she cites Fatmagül Berktay, *Tek Tanrılı Dinler Karşısında Kadın: Hıristiyanlıkta ve İslamiyette Kadının Statüsüne Karşılaştırmalı Bir Yaklaşım* (Istanbul: Metis Yayıncılık, 1995), pp.26-27.

15. Tuksal, *Kadın Karşıtı Söylemin İslam Geleneğindeki İzdüşümleri*, pp.33-34.

16. Tuksal, *Kadın Karşıtı Söylemin İslam Geleneğindeki İzdüşümleri*, p.34; the English version of this quotation is taken from Georges Duby, *Love and Marriage in the Middle Ages,* trans. Jane Dunnett (Chicago, IL: University of Chicago Press, 1994), p.196. Tuksal cites a Turkish version: Georges Duby, *Erkek Ortaçağ, Aşka Dair ve Diğer Denemeler,* trans. M. Ali Kılıçbay (Istanbul: Ayrıntı Yayınları, 1991), p.205.

17. Tuksal, *Kadın Karşıtı Söylemin İslam Geleneğindeki İzdüşümleri*, p.34. Traditional Hadith scholars, on the other hand, considered their attempt at objectivity to be the greatest strength of their methodology.

18. Tuksal, *Kadın Karşıtı Söylemin İslam Geleneğindeki İzdüşümleri*, p.42.

19. Fazlur Rahman, *Islam and Modernity: The Transformation of an Intellectual Tradition* (Chicago, IL: University of Chicago Press, 1982), p.20.

20. Safet Bektovic, 'Towards a neo-modernist Islam: Fazlur Rahman and the rethinking of Islamic tradition and modernity', *Studia Theologica – Nordic Journal of Theology* 70(2) (2016), p.164.

21. Aysha A. Hidayatullah, *Feminist Edges of the Qur'an* (Oxford: Oxford University Press, 2014), p.31.

22. Tuksal, *Kadın Karşıtı Söylemin İslam Geleneğindeki İzdüşümleri*, p.47.

23. Ibid., *Kadın Karşıtı Söylemin İslam Geleneğindeki İzdüşümleri*, p.47.

24. Literally, "example" (*örnek*).
25. The word "*doku*" has a range of meanings in Turkish, such as biological "tissue," "texture," or the "fabric" or structure of something in a metaphorical sense (as in the English, "social fabric"). Tuksal uses the term in the metaphorical sense and associates it with weaving. Thus, the English term "fabric" has been chosen here to translate Tuksal's specific metaphorical usage of the term.
26. Tuksal, *Kadın Karşıtı Söylemin İslam Geleneğindeki İzdüşümleri*, p.51.
27. Literally, "the human being."
28. Tuksal, *Kadın Karşıtı Söylemin İslam Geleneğindeki İzdüşümleri*, pp.48-49; All Qur'anic translations are taken from Seyyed Hossein Nasr, Caner K. Dagli, Maria Massi Dakake, Joseph E. B. Lumbard, and Mohammed Rustom (eds.), *The Study Quran: A New Translation and Commentary* (New York: HarperCollins, 2015).
29. Tuksal, *Kadın Karşıtı Söylemin İslam Geleneğindeki İzdüşümleri*, pp.50-51.
30. Ibid., *Kadın Karşıtı*, p.51.
31. Ibid., *Kadın Karşıtı*, p.50.
32. Ibid., *Kadın Karşıtı*, p.48.
33. Ibid., *Kadın Karşıtı*, p.46.
34. Ibid., *Kadın Karşıtı*, p.48.
35. Ibid., *Kadın Karşıtı*, p.48.
36. Ibid., *Kadın Karşıtı*, p.71.
37. Ibid., *Kadın Karşıtı*, pp.71, 277.
38. Ibid., *Kadın Karşıtı*, pp.67-68.
39. Sa'adiyya Shaikh, 'Knowledge, Women, and Gender in the Hadith: A Feminist Interpretation', *Islam and Christian-Muslim Relations* 15(1) (2004), p.100.
40. Shaikh, 'Knowledge, Women, and Gender in the Hadith', p.99.
41. Ziba Mir-Hosseini, 'Muslim Legal Tradition and the Challenge of Gender Equality', in *Men in Charge? Rethinking Male Authority in Muslim Legal Tradition*, eds. Ziba Mir-Hosseini, Mulki Al-Sharmani, and Jana Rumminger (Oxford: Oneworld, 2015), p.14.
42. Mir-Hosseini, 'Muslim Legal Tradition', p.37.
43. Kecia Ali, *Sexual Ethics and Islam* (2nd edn. Oxford: Oneworld, 2016), pp.187-88.
44. Ayesha S. Chaudhry, *Domestic Violence and the Islamic Tradition: Ethics, Law, and the Muslim Discourse on Gender* (Oxford: Oxford University Press, 2013), pp.7-8.
45. Chaudhry, *Domestic Violence and the Islamic Tradition*, p.11.
46. Karen Bauer, *Gender Hierarchy in the Qur'an: Medieval Interpretations, Modern Responses* (Cambridge: Cambridge University Press, 2015), p.166.
47. Bauer, *Gender Hierarchy in the Qur'an*, pp.7, 24-5, 33.
48. Chaudhry, *Domestic Violence and the Islamic Tradition*, p.182; Mir-Hosseini, 'Muslim Legal Tradition', pp.19-22, 25, 31.
49. Ali, *Sexual Ethics and Islam*, pp.193-94.
50. amina wadud, *Inside the Gender Jihad: Women's Reform in Islam* (Oxford: Oneworld, 2006), p.192.
51. wadud, *Inside the Gender Jihad*, pp.204-5.
52. wadud, *Inside the Gender Jihad*, p.197.
53. wadud, *Inside the Gender Jihad*, p.213; amina wadud, 'The Ethics of Tawhid over the Ethics of Qiwamah', in *Men in Charge? Rethinking Male Authority in Muslim Legal Tradition*, eds. Ziba Mir-Hosseini, Mulki Al-Sharmani, and Jana Rumminger (Oxford: Oneworld, 2015), p.266.

54. wadud, 'The Ethics of Tawhid over the Ethics of Qiwamah', p.270.
55. wadud, 'The Ethics of Tawhid over the Ethics of Qiwamah', pp.272-73.
56. Bektovic, 'Towards a neo-modernist Islam', p.166.
57. Chaudhry, *Domestic Violence and the Islamic Tradition*, pp.3-4, 27; Hidayatullah, *Feminist Edges of the Qur'an*, p.137.
58. Chaudhry, *Domestic Violence and the Islamic Tradition*, p.3.
59. Chaudhry, *Domestic Violence and the Islamic Tradition*, pp.3-4.
60. Hidayatullah, *Feminist Edges of the Qur'an*, pp.152-53.
61. Hidayatullah, *Feminist Edges of the Qur'an*, p.194.

Bibliography

Aksoy, Hürcan Aslı, 'Invigorating Democracy in Turkey: The Agency of Organized Islamist Women', *Politics and Gender* 11 (2015), pp.146-170.

Ali, Kecia, *Sexual Ethics and Islam*, 2nd edn. Oxford: Oneworld, 2016.

Arat, Yeşim, 'Islamist Women and Feminist Concerns in Contemporary Turkey', *Frontiers* 37(3) (2016), pp.125-50.

Bauer, Karen, *Gender Hierarchy in the Qur'an: Medieval Interpretations, Modern Responses*. Cambridge: Cambridge University Press, 2015.

Berktay, Fatmagül, *Tek Tanrılı Dinler Karşısında Kadın: Hıristiyanlıkta ve İslamiyette Kadının Statüsüne Karşılaştırmalı Bir Yaklaşım*. Istanbul: Metis Yayıncılık, 1995.

Chaudhry, Ayesha A, *Domestic Violence and the Islamic Tradition: Ethics, Law, and the Muslim Discourse on Gender*. Oxford: Oxford University Press, 2013.

Dorroll, Philip, 'Post-Gezi Islamic Theology: Intersectional Islamic Feminism in Turkey', *Review of Middle East Studies* 50(2) (2017), pp.157-171.

Duby, Georges, *Love and Marriage in the Middle Ages*, trans. Jane Dunnett. Chicago, IL: University of Chicago Press, 1994.

——, *Erkek Ortaçağ, Aşka Dair ve Diğer Denemeler*, trans. M. Ali Kılıçbay. Istanbul: Ayrıntı Yayınları, 1991.

Hidayatullah, Aysha A, *Feminist Edges of the Qur'an*. Oxford: Oxford University Press, 2014.

Jelen, Brigitte, 'Educated, independent, and covered: The professional aspirations and experiences of university-educated hijabi in contemporary Turkey'. *Women's Studies International Forum* 34 (2011), pp.308-19.

Korteweg, Anna C. and Gökçe Yurdakul, *The Headscarf Debates: Conflicts of National Belonging*. Palo Alto, CA: Stanford University Press, 2014.

Lerner, Gerda, *The Creation of Patriarchy*. Oxford: Oxford University Press, 1986.

Mir-Hosseini, Ziba, 'Muslim Legal Tradition and the Challenge of Gender Equality', in *Men in Charge? Rethinking Authority in the Muslim Legal Tradition*, eds. Ziba Mir-Hosseini, Mulki Al-Sharmani, and Jana Rumminger. Oxford: Oneworld, 2015, pp.13-43.

Nasr, Seyyed Hossein, Caner K. Dagli, Maria Massi Dakake, Joseph E. B. Lumbard, and Mohammed Rustom (eds.), *The Study Quran: A New Translation and Commentary*. New York: HarperCollins, 2015.

Rahman, Fazlur, *Islam and Modernity: Transformation of an Intellectual Tradition*. Chicago, IL: University of Chicago Press, 1982.

Shaikh, Sa'diyya. 'Knowledge, Women, and Gender in the Hadith: A Feminist Interpretation', *Islam and Christian-Muslim Relations* 15(1) (2004), pp.99-108.

Tajali, Mona, 'Islamic Women's Groups and the Quest for Political Representation in Turkey and Iran', *The Middle East Journal* 69(4) (2015), pp.563-81.

Tuksal, Hidayet Şefkatli, 'Adalet bekliyoruz!' *Serbestiyet*, January 19, 2017, http://serbestiyet.com/yazarlar/hidayet-s.-tuksal/adalet-bekliyoruz-755441.

___, *Kadın Karşıtı Söylemin İslam Geleneğindeki İzdüşümleri*. Ankara: Kitabiyat Yayinları, 2000; OTTO Yayinları 2014.

___, 'Misogynistic Reports in the Hadith Literature', in *Muslima Theology: The Voices of Muslim Women Theologians*, eds. Ednan Aslan, Marcia Hermansen, and Elif Medeni. Frankfurt am Main: Peter Lang, 2013, pp.133-154.

___, 'OHAL'de hukuka riayet', *Serbestiyet*, February 11, 2017, http://serbestiyet.com/yazarlar/hidayet-s.-tuksal/ohalde-hukuka-riayet-762655.

___, 'Türkler Suriyelilerle birlikte yaşamaya hazır görünmüyor', *Hürriyet*, May 10, 2018, http://www.hurriyet.com.tr/turkler-suriyelilerle-birlikte-yasamaya-hazir-40832069.

wadud, amina, *Inside the Gender Jihad: Women's Reform in Islam*. Oxford: Oneworld, 2006.

___, 'The Ethics of Tawhid Over the Ethics of Qiwamah', in *Men in Charge? Rethinking Authority in the Muslim Legal Tradition*, eds. Ziba Mir-Hosseini, Mulki Al-Sharmani, and Jana Rumminger. Oxford: Oneworld, 2015, pp.256-274.

4

Islamic Jurisprudence in Iran: Traditionalism, Reformism and Gender Justice

Samaneh Oladi

The contemporary legal status of Iranian women is a complex and contentious topic that has engaged the ulema in a dynamic debate. This chapter begins with the contested issue of religious authority and knowledge, and addresses the prospects and constraints faced by religious scholars seeking gender justice within the Shiʿite tradition. In the second section I examine various strands of Islamic jurisprudence (*fiqh*) employed by these religious scholars. I underscore several factors that differentiate the traditionalist approach to gender justice from their reformist counterparts. In particular, the jurisprudential and hermeneutical methods employed by reformist ulema highlights their ethical considerations. The next section further analyzes whether adherence to dynamic jurisprudence can advance egalitarian principles in the Shiʿite tradition and ultimately contends that it is an effective means of democratizing religious interpretation.

Religious Authority and Knowledge

According to the Islamic tradition, religious authority is mainly based on having religious knowledge in conjunction with piety. Prophets gained their authority based on divine revelation (*waḥy*) that signifies their infallible knowledge.[1] For the believers, after the death of Prophet Muhammad, divine revelation ended. In the post-revelation interlude, pious individuals continued to cultivate a distinct relationship with God through reflection on the meaning of divine revelation. These individuals were accredited with an idiosyncratic kind of religious status that moved beyond conventional perceptions of authority.[2]

In sacred Islamic scriptures, it is difficult to confine the understanding of religious authority to a single word. The Qur'anic phrase *ulū al-amr* (those who possess authority) in verse 4:59 has at times been interpreted as exclusively political authority by Sunnite Muslims. However, according to the Islamicist Wadad Kadi, the authority with which the Qur'an is generally concerned is religious.[3] When looking at early commentators such as Mujāhid b. Jabr (d. 102/720), among the necessary qualifications for the *ulū al-amr* is to have religious knowledge, and the ability to perform *ijtihād* (independent reasoning).[4] These scholars contend that *ulū al-amr* is a direct reference to ulema, who have insightful knowledge about religion and possess the ability to engage in legal reasoning. By contrast, later generations of exegetes, represented by al-Ṭabarī (d. 310/923), regard the phrase *ulū al-amr* as a reference to possessors of political authority so long as their commands are not contradictory to the teachings of the Qur'an.[5] According to Kadi, the transition from initial non-political interpretations of this phrase to a political one reflects societal change.[6] Furthermore, the differing interpretation of the Qur'anic phrase *ulū al-amr* in diverse sociopolitical contexts is indication that the perception of religious and political authority varied in different historical and social milieus.[7]

In the Islamic tradition, legitimate leadership and authority are derived from moral excellence and precedence. Each concept espouses a particular discourse on leadership and both are critical within Sunnite–Shiᶜite polemic.[8] In the second century following the advent of Islam, the Shiᶜites advanced a notion of *ulū al-amr* that synthesized political and religious authority. Shiᶜite scholars articulated that the Ahl al-Bayt (People of the House of Prophet Muhammad), through his daughter Fatimah, were chosen to be Imams by God's decree. As such, Asma Afsaruddin argues that in classical Shiᶜite works, the Imams are depicted as the true *ulū al-amr* whose religious authority is based on their knowledge of esoteric sciences.[9] In view of this conviction, only the Imams can be in custody of such knowledge due to their lineage and proximity to Muhammad. The Shiᶜites believe that the Imams, because of their infallible knowledge, are the rightful leaders and authorities. Afsaruddin reiterates that the Shiᶜite Imams must be infallible, possess knowledge of the other world, and that God must designate their position. The Imams, similar to prophets, are considered to be infallible leaders who possess distinctive qualities including morality and piety. They differ from prophets in that they do not receive revelation, but their interpretation and knowledge of the Qur'an is considered to be reliable and irrefutable. In fact, Shiᶜites believe that only Imams are capable of grasping the inner meaning of sacred scriptures.[10]

Obtaining the status of a religious authority within the Shiᶜite tradition is an intricate task. A number of Qur'anic verses denote that some individuals apart from prophets may be endowed with a measure of special knowledge and understanding.[11] For Sunnites these verses refer to those who acquire religious scholarship. In particular, the term *awliyā'* (saints) is perceived to refer to the first four caliphs and then all the other companions of the Prophet. Shiᶜites similarly believe that ulema are bestowed with special knowledge. However, their conceptualization of *awliyā'* is different in that they consider these verses to be a reference to infallible Imams. According to Shiᶜite conviction, religiosity in its authentic form is found in sacred scriptures and in the Prophet's teachings as well as the Prophet's household. For Shiᶜites, the event of Ghadīr Khumm, which took place on 18 Dhū al-Hijjah 10/632, is a significant historic moment. During his sermon on this day, the Prophet stated, "He whose master (*mawlā*) I am, ᶜAlī is his master". As Faud Khuri points out, Shiᶜites interpret this hadith to mean that the Prophet appointed ᶜAlī as his successor. Considering that the Prophet is believed to be an infallible messenger, the nomination of ᶜAlī as his successor signifies God's decree.[12]

The belief in the doctrine of imamate has led to the creation of several distinct categories of religious specialization and hierarchy in Shiᶜism. The question of religious and political authority of the Shiᶜite community in the absence of the last Imam, Muḥammad al-Mahdī, who went into complete occultation in 329/941, resulted in a more prominent role for the ulema, who in effect began to fill in this gap of leadership.[13] Within the Shiᶜite scholarly community, ulema are classified according to their scholarly ranking. The two main categories are mullas and ayatollahs.

Mullas specialize in the history and rituals of Islam, particularly rituals that recount the history of the Imams and commemorate their death. Such rituals highlight brutalities committed by ruling elites against Shiᶜite Imams, particularly al-Ḥusayn, and play an important part in the Shiᶜite community.[14] Mullas also attempt to relate historical events to modern issues. The title ayatollah originally was granted to the highest-ranking ulema. This title is applied to scholars who have attained the rank of *ijtihād* and are able to act as *marājiᶜ al-taqlīd* (sources of emulation). The term ayatollah is at times interchangeable with *mujtahid* within Shiᶜite circles.[15] These individuals are meticulously trained in religious seminaries and are able to undertake independent legal reasoning. According to Rainer Brunner, when Qom became a main learning center for Shiʿites in the 1920s, the consolidation of learning augmented the number of ayatollahs, which resulted in further classification of their scholarly merits. Thus, the highest ranking and the most prestigious religious authorities were granted the title of *ayatollah al-ozma*. This title is used interchangeably with *marjaʿ al-taqlīd*.[16] These *marājiʿ* deal with legal issues that play a significant role and influence in the social and political realms of Shiʿite society.[17]

Although the *marājiʿ* cannot replace the Shiʿite Imams, they are held in the highest esteem in religious circles. The idea that the ulema are heirs to the prophets is conveyed in a famous hadith, which is accepted by Shiʿite traditionalists such as Muḥammad b. Yaʿqūb al-Kulaynī (d. 329/941).[18] This admiration for knowledge cultivated the rise of an independent group of scholars and the view that believers should follow these learned scholars, a process that is termed *taqlīd*. The ulema thus began to constitute a distinct category in Shiʿite Islam due to their level of religious knowledge.[19] According to Brunner, this became even more pronounced in the aftermath of the Iranian Revolution in 1979, which led to the establishment of a state that was governed by high-ranking ulema. It is in this spirit that Ayatollah Khomeini, in his book *The Islamic Government*, adduces several hadiths in support of his contention that the ulema are fit to rule in the absence of the twelfth Shiʿite Imam.[20] Khomeini's reliance on the notion of *welayat-e faqih* (the mandate of the jurist) greatly impacted the dynamic of religious and political authority in Shiʿite Iran.[21]

Religious and political authority in Shiʿite tradition is based primarily on the possession of knowledge of religious matters, combined with personal piety. The Arabic words that convey the meaning of knowledge are *ʿilm*, *maʿrifah*, and *fiqh*, among others. Generally, *ʿilm* is understood as a broad term for knowledge that can be religious or secular.[22] Islamic religious sciences are divided into several important strands, which consist of exegesis and the study of traditions among others. The most imperative religious science is *fiqh*, which is the attempt to understand God's law, and its practitioners are referred to as *fuqahā'*.

Thus, legal scholars are a division of the ulema.[23] The term *fiqh* (understanding or acquiring knowledge) came to mean Islamic law in religious discourses. Ibn ʿAbd al-Barr (d. 463/1071) also referenced this point in his book *Jāmiʿ bayān al- ʿilm*, where he pointed out that jurists often equated *ʿilm* with *fiqh* and used the terms interchangeably.[24]

The Sunnite and Shiᶜite traditions offer a comparable understanding of *ᶜilm*. According to Charles Butterworth, *ᶜilm* constitutes for Sunnites the basis of Islam itself. While secular fields have been included in the definition of *ᶜilm,* they are considered inferior to religious sciences. The Sunnite tradition understands *ᶜilm* in relation to legal knowledge with two categories.[25] The first category is referred to as "general knowledge," which can be found in the sacred scriptures. The second type of knowledge is alluded to as "particular knowledge," which is limited to qualified ulema. Due to their training in Islamic legal thought and tradition, the ulema are able to extract laws and formulate specific rulings.[26]

Shiᶜite tradition, similar to its Sunnite counterpart, understands *ᶜilm* to be mainly religious knowledge. Shiᶜite jurists, such as Ibn al-Muṭahhar al-Ḥillī (d. 726/1325), classified knowledge into two main categories, which include "certain knowledge" and "uncertain knowledge".[27] In Islamic thought, certain knowledge is based on irrefutable proof that is not susceptible to uncertainty, whereas uncertain knowledge is based on tentative evidence with its legitimacy dependent upon the authorization of the ulema. Butterworth avers that the majority of Shiᶜite scholars understand *ᶜilm* as parallel to *ᶜaql* (intellect). They regard intellect as judgment – one can know by it which acts are considered moral, and which are considered immoral.[28]

Similar to the Muᶜtazilite theory of knowledge, application of the intellect is of significance in the Shiᶜite tradition. Shiᶜites believe that the knowledge that God is omnipotent and the supreme Creator is understood by humans through reason, irrespective of revelation. The role of revelation is to confirm and supplement what is already recognized by human reason and rationale.[29] From this premise, Shiᶜites, like the Muᶜtazilite school of theology, posit that the decrees of God are accessible to rational thought. They further argue that because knowledge is derived from reason, the faculty of reason is the definitive authority in distinguishing moral acts from immoral acts.[30]

Justice in Shiᶜite Theology and Jurisprudence

Justice (*ᶜadl*) figures prominently in the Shiᶜite tradition as one of its primary principles and is regarded as the essence of all religious teachings. The principle of *ᶜadl* is of great significance in Shiᶜite theology, and it plays a central part in the advancement of its jurisprudence. The word *ᶜadl*, which means to act equitably and justly, is also used to convey the idea of making two things equal.[31] In Shiᶜism, it is essential to believe that justice must prevail and exist at all stages. Shiᶜite theologians consider good and bad as objective and, as such, rational criteria can be used for moral judgements. Consequently, God is both just and removed from committing an evil act, and human beings can rationally understand this.

Shiᶜite thought relies on reason to infer that God does not resort to injustice because injustice is thought to be an imperfection. Shiᶜite theologians and philosophers consider God as the perfect being. Since justice is a quality attributed to perfection, God therefore must act within a just framework. Numerous references in the Qur'an emphasize God's inclination towards justice.[32] Divine justice is not restricted to merely the theological aspect of Shiᶜism, as the issue is seen as a fundamental aspect of the Islamic religion. Moreover, Shiᶜite scholars have attempted to advocate for social, political and economic justice, reflecting its place as one of the most significant jurisprudential precepts in Shiᶜism.[33]

Shiᶜites, along with Sunnite Muᶜtazilites and Māturīdites believe that morality and immorality are objective, emphasizing rationality for moral decisions. They believe in the inherent morality and immorality of actions, holding that humans have free will and are therefore liable for their actions. A major distinction between the Muᶜtazilite and Shiᶜite beliefs is in the delegation of divine power. According to Mohammad Shomali, the Muᶜtazilites believe that God has entrusted his authority over human actions to them and they possess the ability to control their deeds (*qadar*). The Shiᶜites, on the other hand, hold the view that while determinism is against divine justice, and that humans have free will, their autonomy is restricted, as God has total authority upon humans.[34] This point is mentioned in a hadith attributed to Jaᶜfar al-Sadiq: "There is no compulsion, nor is there absolute delegation of power, but the real position is between the two extremes."[35]

Reason is one of the main sources of Shiᶜite jurisprudence. In this context, reason is defined as a categorical judgment informed by practical and pure reason. As Hossein Modarressi states, practical reason can tell us that justice is ethical and injustice is unethical. This view informs Shiᶜite jurisprudence in the position that whatever is condoned by reason is also condoned by religion. Based on this principle, religious rules may be inferred directly from reason. It is in this context that Shiᶜite Imams urged their followers to use reason and logic in both theology and jurisprudence.[36] The nature of reason can be determined by "the understanding" and prevalent logic "among the most knowledgeable people of the time," including the ulema.[37]

Unlike the Shiᶜite school of thought that emphasizes rationalism, many Sunnites who adhere to Ashᶜarite theology give greater precedence to revelation than reason. Ashᶜarites hold the position that the knowledge of moral and immoral acts does not depend on human reason but on the decree of God, which is recognized through revelation.[38] To the Ashᶜarites there are no objective criteria for acts that are moral or immoral, as they believe God's actions and commands are just. They further undermine human free will by emphasizing God's role in creating humans as vessels of divine acts.[39] The Shiᶜites, on the other hand, argue that the notion of justice is inherent and has a logical foundation, and prevails independently of religious texts. This arguably allows Shiᶜite theology more hermeneutical flexibility than the position adopted by Ashᶜarites. Despite this difference in the understanding of the role of rationality in interpreting scripture, it is noteworthy that most contemporary reformers highlight the important role of the intellect in developing religious rulings.[40] Thus contemporary reformist thought in the Muslim world both in the Shiᶜite and Sunnite context has often taken the form of neo-Muᶜtazilism.[41] For neo-Muᶜtazilites, the school's focus on inherent human moral knowledge and desire to subject interpretation to rational criteria fit well with their reform agenda.

The methodologies for dynamic jurisprudence in Shiᶜism rest on the reinterpretation of traditional Islamic scripture, a process known as *ijtihād*.[42] Although as a legal term *ijtihād* has a distinct definition, both Sunnite and Shiᶜite writers agree with al-Hilli's description, which defines *ijtihād* as "expending of one's utmost effort in the inquiry into legal questions admitting of only probable answers."[43] Shiᶜite jurists did not, however, always adhere to the notion of *ijtihād*. According to Hossein Modarressi, up until the sixth/twelfth century, Shiᶜites mainly abstained from the use of the concept. However, after the twelfth Imam disappeared in the late third/ninth century, there was the beginning of a greater acceptance of *ijtihād*, and it grew to be one of the central methods through which legal issues were addressed.[44] *Ijtihād* in Shiᶜite tradition has two fundamental ramifications: on the one hand, it requires believers to abide by the ulema and to emulate the most learned scholar. On the other hand, the ulema must pursue a set of procedures to ascertain the identity of the most learned scholar and acknowledge the resulting internal hierarchy.[45]

The legitimacy of *ijtihād* and its appropriate scope have long been the object of extensive discussion between both Sunnite and Shiᶜite scholars. Some Sunnite scholars, unlike their Shiᶜite counterparts, believed that the "gate of *ijtihād*" had been closed since the fourth/tenth century. However, Wael Hallaq argues that contrary to this prevalent conception, the "gate of *ijtihād*" never fully closed. During the turn of the seventeenth century, Sunnite Muslim reformers began to disapprove of imitation (*taqlīd*), which is to follow a *mujtahid* in religious laws. At the same time, they promoted greater use of *ijtihād* by individuals outside of the traditional religious hierarchy. The reformist movements of the nineteenth century emerged among Muslim thinkers such as Jamāl al-Dīn al-Afghānī and Muhammad ᶜAbduh, who wanted to return to the rationalism of the Muᶜtazilites.[46] Among Sunnite scholars, contemporary proponents of *ijtihād* may share commonalities with the reformers of the nineteenth century, but they differ in relation to the scope of their intellectual horizons. Whereas the early advocates of *ijtihād* worked within an Islamic framework, today's reformists combine knowledge of Islamic learning and scripture with secular training.[47]

There are currently two camps of scholars that are spearheading reform in Shiᶜite Iran. The first group are those who argue that the conventional Islamic tradition is no longer applicable to the challenges of, and changes within, contemporary Muslim lives. This camp permits reformers to propose their own interpretations as appropriate responses to present needs and focuses on the Qur'an to the detriment of the Imāmite tradition. Scholars following this approach argue that the Qur'an is situated in a specific time and place and therefore should be reinterpreted by each generation in order to stay pertinent to the realities of the Shiᶜite community.[48] The second group of reformist scholars are similar to their Sunnite counterparts and they have attempted to incorporate aspects of the classical tradition rather than dismissing it altogether.[49] These scholars combine traditional Islamic scholarship with dynamic jurisprudence when extracting legal rulings.

Islamic Jurisprudence: Fiqh-e Taqlidi and Fiqh-e Pouya

The necessity to establish new jurisprudence capable of tackling contemporary issues gave rise to a pluralistic approach in the Islamic Republic of Iran. There are two types of jurisprudence (*fiqh*) that are employed by ulema and perpetuated by religious scholars. The first type is traditional jurisprudence (*fiqh-e taqlīdī*), which continues to promote orthodox principles and enjoys the backing of traditionalist ulema. For the traditionalists, *ijtihād* is perceived as a practice involving juristic reasoning to derive legal rulings on issues where primary sources including the Qur'an, Sunnah of the Prophet, Imams, and earlier jurists have remained silent. Essentially, a traditionalist outlook on *fiqh* restricts independent reasoning and limits the right to interpret sacred texts. Proponents of *fiqh-e taqlīdī* confine the use of reasoning to cases that have not been addressed by previous jurists or religious texts.

The second type is dynamic jurisprudence (*fiqh-e pouya*) that, while true to Islamic tradition, attempts to revitalize the legal pluralism of Shiʿism. Reformist ulema and activists who represent a rational yet tradition-informed movement of jurisprudential thought in contemporary Iran employ this strand of jurisprudence. Such a jurisprudential approach, versions of which are prevalent amongst both Shiʿite and Sunnite reformists, encompasses rational thinking through an epistemology that foregrounds justice. As Islamic reformers, they are interested in presenting a dynamic understanding of Islam by employing *fiqh-e pouya* as a means to articulate a more egalitarian and modern understanding of Islamic legal tradition. The reformation of legal rulings with regards to gender justice is at the heart of this movement.

Fiqh-e Taqlīdī and Gender Justice

The contested issue of gender equality has invoked various responses from both reformist and traditionalist ulema. The traditionalists who adhere to *fiqh-e taqlīdī*, do not endorse equality for men and women. These ulema issue religious rulings based on their particular understanding of the world in a manner that may lend itself to gender hierarchy. In this respect, Islam is similar to other religions in that it possesses its own internal logic for different religious rulings. As reformist scholar Mohsen Kadivar argues, under this conception the Islamic tradition encompasses specific rights in which religion, gender, and certain beliefs have priority over the human rights of individuals. Consequently, the value of equality cannot merge with the rights regime that exists in traditional Islamic jurisprudence.[50]

Most individuals who adhere to *fiqh-e taqlīdī* believe the contradiction that exists between Islamic law and gender equality is inevitable and therefore subject to rejection.[51] Traditionalists believe that the difference in the rulings concerning men and women are not an indication that men are valued more than women. It is in fact the inherent distinction between men and women that lead to their different rulings. While acknowledging the equality of men and women before God, these traditionalists argue that it is the biological, physical, and emotional differences between the sexes that lead to different religious rulings. Traditional jurists caution against misconstruing the concept of equality of rights with the sameness of rights in lieu of the responsibilities men and women have to undertake in traditional families and societies.[52]

Traditionalists define gender justice in terms of the enactment of Islamic law. According to these ulema, the different religious rulings pertaining to men and women stem from their inherent differences. Hence, acknowledging these differences is not an indication that Islamic law is unjust towards women. These differences account for the notion of complementarity in gender relations both in public and private spheres. Some traditionalists argue that there are differences between men and women:

> Not in their rights but in the duties of each sex, stemming from differing abilities and the natural division of labor. Others have tried to explain this disparity by connecting differences in rights to physical, psychological, and spiritual differences between the sexes.[53]

Accordingly, these scholars make a case against the claim that equality in legal rights advances the position of women. They argue, for example, that absolute equality in Islamic family law could undermine women's negotiating power in marriage. Moreover, the claim of women to maintenance and dower (*mahr*) within the confines of the family would be eliminated if absolute equality were to be enforced.[54] Traditionalists caution against the difficult socio-economic situation women might face in the absence of such financial support.

Traditionalist scholars such as Mohammad Reza Zibaei Nejad also maintain that men and women excel at different types of tasks and, as such, argue that insisting on an egalitarian framework is not in line with the teachings of the Qur'an and Sunnah of the Prophet and Imams. They contend that the Qur'an does not view men and women in a similar fashion, yet it upholds their dignity far more than secularism. These jurists believe that it is a materialist outlook on life that endorses a cultural model affording women identical social status. Thus, women may be glorified at a superficial level in secular societies but in the long term it is men who will benefit from such a cultural model.[55] Traditionalists, therefore, argue that despite women's participation in the workforce, the burden of caregiving and domestic responsibilities falls on the shoulders of women who struggle to merge the ideas of being ideal mothers and employees.

There is apprehension among traditionalists regarding the critique of gender roles. They argue that by depicting the discrepancy in gender roles as a sign of discrimination, reformists generate doubt in the public's mind about the validity of the classical Islamic ruling on this issue.[56] They further stress that, in the midst of defending women's rights, religious values are undermined and replaced with irreligious norms. In Islam, which considers humans to be God's representatives on this earth, the value of human beings is not based on having equal rights, but rather their deeds. The traditionalists argue that instead of ignoring these God-given differences, the reformists should focus their attention on the constructive and complementary differences that exist between men and women and interpret these differences as distinctive means to achieve perfection.

Traditionalist jurists, such as Ayatollah Javadi Amoli, are weary of the reformists' attempts to base their arguments heavily on the verses of the Qur'an and human reason without much attention to the Hadith of the Prophet and Imams.[57] The traditionalists argue that the rulings of Islamic law have to be based on Islamic principles and in consensus with the narrations of the Shiʿite Imams. Furthermore, they contend that the concept of justice is a static notion, not influenced by the custom (*ʿurf*) of society. Hence, it is not acceptable to claim that since a segment of a population is not in agreement with a particular divine law, the law itself is unjust. Traditionalist ulema caution the reformist exegetes to not blindly adhere to secular principles that make equality necessary for justice.

The controversy surrounding the notion of gender justice is found not only among the legal opinions of ulema, but also within the verses of the Qur'an and the Hadith. Some of the juristic opinions and sacred texts have been shown to be incompatible with contemporary standards for gender equality. Thus, from the stance of traditionalists, gender equality that seeks equal individual rights for men and women is anti-Islamic in nature and in violation of the teachings of Islam. The resulting discord between gender equality norms and what traditional Islamic jurisprudence considers as unyielding legal principles inherently lends itself to gender hierarchy.[58]

For the most part, traditionalists contend that the divergence between traditional exegesis and the modern framework for gender equality should not be overlooked. Despite such conflicts these scholars believe that traditional Islamic jurisprudence is capable of offering alternatives to contemporary gender equality policies.[59] Mohsen Kadivar states that the last two centuries have witnessed the development of Shiʿite jurisprudence after newly developed principles were introduced by ulema such as Shaykh Murtada Ansari (d. 1864). Of such principles is the notion of "secondary precepts", which allow for amendment in the case of exceptional circumstances.[60] There are several principles within these secondary precepts that can be applied to change discriminatory legal rulings.[61] However, in reality, these principles are not applied in normal situations and cannot effectively address the points of conflict identified by reformists.

Fiqh-e Pouya and Gender Justice

In contrast to the traditionalists, reformist ulema are interested in the dynamic aspect of the Islamic tradition. Such reformist scholars are both a reaction to modernity and a product of modernization and globalization.[62] A number of scholars, such as Ziba Mir-Hosseini, have argued that the reform movement grew out of the inability of the traditionalist approach to meet the needs and demands of modern society. The drive towards *fiqh-e pouya* in Iran was an attempt to reinterpret Islamic law by considering various factors including human intellect as well as the reason for revelation. The founder of the Islamic Republic of Iran, Ayatollah Khomeini, although initially unpopular, informally initiated the modern reformist movement. Despite its modest beginnings, it gradually found a strong base among religious scholars and the general public. Since the 1990s, *fiqh-e pouya* has gained momentum among reformist ulema such as the ayatollahs Ebrahim Janati, Muhammad Mousavi Bojnourdi, Ahmad Ghabel, and Yusef Saanei.[63] This approach is also becoming increasingly popular among reformist intellectuals and activists.

Adherents to *fiqh-e pouya* believe that critical reinterpretation of the principles found in sacred sources is central for legal reform. They propose a shift from traditional views regarding the inflexibility of Islamic law as understood by traditionalists. In this endeavor, the proponents of *fiqh-e pouya* have met considerable resistance from the advocates of traditional jurisprudence. Although the traditionalists have monopolized the political and religious institutions in Iran, the reformists have consistently gained ground in the realm of legal tradition. The traditionalists' disapproval of the reformists' critical outlook on jurisprudential theories has not deterred their efforts. Reformist scholars do not confine themselves to the judgments of previous jurists. As Ayatollah Bojnourdi argues:

> If a *faqīh* believes that the *fuqahā'* from the past were more knowledgeable and pious than the contemporary *fuqahā'*, then this type of thinking would prevent them from exercising *ijtihād*. Consequently, instead of performing *ijtihād*, they would spend their time defending and proving the accuracy of the opinion of the *mujtahids* of the past. Given that the door of *ijtihād* is open in Shiʿism, it is forbidden for a *mujtahid* to *taqlīd* (imitate) another *mujtahid*.[66]

Thus, a *faqīh* is encouraged to practice *ijtihād* independent of previous legal rulings.[67] If traditionalist ulema and activists persist on conventional paradigms and refuse to break free from their dependency on *mujtahids* of the past, they are likely to find themselves irrelevant to the demands of modern societies. It is essential to remember that the consensus of previous *mujtahids* was reached within a particular time and place. Therefore, jurists living in modern times need to arrive at rulings that are appropriate for society's needs.

The ulema who endorse *fiqh-e pouya* question the practicality of traditional jurisprudential methods without rejecting them entirely. These scholars are interested in offering an alternative method within the broader tradition of Islamic knowledge. They emphasize dynamic jurisprudence as a means of coming to terms with the demands of modernity and globalization of the Muslim world.[68] By highlighting the dynamic nature of Shariʿah found in its classical representation, these reformists seek to pave the way for the reinterpretation of Islamic rulings. By recognizing the imperfection of human effort to capture divine intent, these reformists call for the reassessment of discriminatory laws. This recognition enables individuals to adhere to the principles of their faith while also seeking to restore the long-neglected principles of justice and rationality, which were fundamental tenets of classical Shiʿite jurisprudence.

While criticizing some traditionalists' rigid interpretation of religious texts, reformist scholars offer an alternative method of reading Qur'anic verses and the Hadith of the Prophet and Imams. By considering the context of the Qur'anic revelation, the reformists advocate for a more nuanced interpretation of the intent behind the divine rulings in the Qur'an and Hadith. The reformists support the use of *fiqh-e pouya* by referencing the renowned Shiʿite book of jurisprudence, *Javaher-al-Kalam,* by Muhammad Hasan Najafi (d. 1850). In this book, Najafi argues that jurists must capture the dynamics of time, context, and place.[69] Reformers advocate the notion of contextuality, and occasion of revelation. Shiʿite reformist scholars, similar to their Sunnite counterparts, have underlined the importance of the social and historical context of Qur'anic revelations along with their commitment to a rational mode of reasoning.[70]

The unique interpretation of the Qur'an offered by reformist intellectuals advances reason and gender justice.[71] In addressing the contested issue of women's rights in Islam, reformists argue that the principles of justice must be given prominence in Islamic rulings over other provisions in Islamic jurisprudence. However, traditionalists rebut these changes on the basis that the consensus of the ulema has already been reached through textual evidence. Reformists such as Mohsen Saidzadeh challenge the traditionalists' approach by reasoning that the rulings of previous *mujtahids* regarding women were influenced by their particular context and worldview. In fact, they urge all the ulema to find the courage to challenge some of the rulings of past *mujtahids*. Therefore, *fiqh* rulings that appear to advance disparity between men and women are viewed as either being misinterpreted or belonging to a particular socio-historical context. In this vein, they argue, it is important to acknowledge that the jurisdiction of *fiqh* is confined to the customs of a particular time, and therefore it is essential to reinterpret principles of *fiqh* in light of new social contexts.[72]

The reformist ulema are critical of legal rulings that reinforce gender hierarchy in contemporary society.[73] To encourage a shift in the direction of gender egalitarianism, these ulema resort to three precepts as they practice dynamic jurisprudence. The first precept is based on the teachings of the Qur'an regarding the importance of religion being easy to follow and not entwined with unnecessary precautions.[74] The second directive stipulates the need for legal dispensations when the implementation of a particular ruling is not compatible with human reasoning and intellect (*ʿaql*).[75] The third rule states that *fiqh* rulings should be in line with the values of justice (*ʿadl*). and morality. In order for any legal ruling to be ethical and valid it should meet these three precepts.

Reformist ulema further argue that the principle of justice forbids individuals from restricting the rights of others. Moreover, the Qur'an denounces the subordination of women through various forms of discrimination. By referencing verses in the Qur'an that highlight the importance of acting in a just manner,[76] these scholars argue that oppression is the consequence of human discrimination. In an attempt to challenge hierarchical hermeneutics of certain Qur'anic verses,[77] reformists provide egalitarian interpretation of contested notion such as *nushūz* (disobedience). Although *nushūz* can be applied to behavior on the part of either spouse, most jurists use it in relation to the wife's responsibilities toward her husband. Reformists argue that when the Qur'an refers to an obedient woman, there is no indication that the obedience is in relation to her husband, rather, obedience should be understood as obedience toward God. Thus, traditionalist jurists who interpret this verse to imply the domination of men over women go against the Islamic principle of justice.

For reformists, rulings derived from the Qur'an have priority over those based on other sources such as the Hadith. These ulema argue that some hadith reports contradict the Qur'an, while others go against human reason. One of the oft-cited narrations that is patronizing towards women is attributed to Imam ᶜAlī b. Abī Ṭālib in *Nahj al-Balagha*, in which he states that women are flawed in faith, and deficient in shares of inheritance and intelligence.[78] As Hamid Mavani states, the rationalization offered for such disparaging claims against women is that Alī made these statements after the Battle of the Camel in 36/656, which was initiated by ᶜĀ'ishah, the wife of Prophet Muhammad, and in which many individuals lost their lives.[79] Reformists argue that these statements should be rejected as unauthentic because they contravene the Qur'anic depiction of women and the principle of justice. Ulema such as Yusef Saanei also reject narrations that are considered to be authentic. For instance, Saanei has fiercely rejected narrations that state women should not be the successor of anyone, because they are perceived as unintelligent. These reformists assert that the message of these narrations goes against the principles of the Qur'an as well as human reasoning.[80] They point to the distinctions between the manner in which the Qur'an speaks of women like the wife of Pharaoh and the Queen of Sheba and the way women are portrayed in other Islamic texts.

The reformists remind the traditional ulema that based on Islamic principles any Hadith narration that is in conflict with the direct teachings of the Qur'an is abrogated.[81] Hamid Mavani argues that such approach is in stark contrast to the opinions of most traditional Shiᶜite scholars, for whom prophetic Hadith, narration of the Imams, and the consensus of ulema appear to have greater significance than the Qur'an. By emphasizing rational thinking, these reformers are drawing on the Shiʿite doctrine that justice and rationality have precedence over any religious rulings issued by ulema. They maintain that justice is an intrinsic concept rooted in intellect (*ʿaql*) and can thus exist without divine revelation.[82]

Dynamic Jurisprudence as a Means Towards Reform

The dynamic contention between reformist and traditionalist ulema continues to cultivate advancement of knowledge in contemporary Iran. *Fiqh-e pouya* has opened a normative space within which the policy of the state and social practices are debated.[83] By embracing a more inclusive perspective of women's rights, reformists have adopted an approach that moves beyond the one offered by secularists in an effort to realize gender justice within existing religious and cultural norms. These religious scholars strive to promote jurisprudential dynamicity in order to advance a culture of egalitarianism that acknowledges women's rights and prohibits discrimination on the basis of gender.[84]

By stressing rational interpretation of sacred scriptures, reformists consider the socio-historical contingency of the sources and the need for interpretations to be relevant to the contemporary Shiʿite community. They are gravitating towards greater emphasis on Qur'anic concepts such as justice while also relying on human reason.[85] In this respect, reformist ulema maintain that certain historical legal rulings are no longer relevant or applicable in the modern era. This form of legal reform, they argue, is possible through *fiqh-e pouya*, which can be attained via a theological and intellectual allegiance.[86] Thus, *fiqh-e pouya* can be incorporated as a method that can change religious rulings in order to make them more compatible with the ideals of gender justice.

Reformist ulema speak with authority about how sacred texts can be effectively interpreted to advance women's rights causes. They maintain that applying traditional rulings to modern issues is not only inappropriate and a source of unnecessary suffering, but also contrary to the core message of the Qur'an and justice. The goal of these scholars is to reform the legal status of women by finding common ground between Islamic legal traditions and modern legal needs in light of the ever-changing social, economic, and political conditions.[87] These scholars recognize the value of incorporating new understandings and ideas into the body of Islamic tradition as a way of not mitigating, but enriching it.

The dynamic jurisprudence advanced by reformists has invoked various hermeneutical principles that have led to lasting reforms in Shiʿite Iran. Reformist ulema merge Islamic methodologies with human rationality and the principle of justice while being firmly grounded in the Islamic tradition. This approach diverts from the method employed by traditionalist ulema that do not view human rationality and justice as central precepts of jurisprudence. Reformists are cognizant of the fact that Iranian society is in a transitional phase and seek to modernize legal rulings without compromising their Islamic identity. Finally, despite their differences, it is important to note that these two strands of jurisprudential tradition are not static categories entirely separate from one another; rather one witnesses a continuing dialogue and discourse among their advocates.

ENDNOTES

1. Asma Afsaruddin, 'The Epistemology of Excellence: Sunni-Shi'i Dialectics on Legitimate Leadership', in *Speaking for Islam: Religious Authorities in Muslim Societies*, eds. Gudrun Krämer and Sabine Schmidtke (Leiden: Brill, 2006), p.49.
2. Afsaruddin, 'The Epistemology of Excellence', p.50.
3. Wadad Kadi, 'Authority', in *Encyclopedia of the Qur'ān*, ed. Jane Dammen McAuliffe (Leiden: Brill, 2001-6).
4. Cited in Asma Afsaruddin, 'Authority, religious', in *Encyclopedia of Islam, Three*, eds. Gudrun Krämer, Denis Matringe, John Nawas, Everett Rowson (Leiden: Brill, 2011).
5. Cited in Kadi, 'Authority'.
6. Kadi, 'Authority'.
7. Ibid., 'Authority'.
8. Asma Afsaruddin, *Excellence and Precedence: Medieval Islamic Discourse on Legitimate Leadership* (Leiden: Brill. 2002), p.27.
9. Afsaruddin, *Excellence and Precedence*.
10. Foud Khuri, 'The Ulama: A Comparative Study of Sunni and Shi'a Religious Officials', *Middle Eastern Studies* 23(3) (1987), pp.291-312.
11. See the following Qur'anic verses: 35:28, 10:62 and 4:69.
12. Khuri, 'The Ulama: A Comparative Study of Sunni and Shi'a Religious Officials', p.303.
13. Mohammad Ali Amir-Moezzi, 'Islam in Iran vii. The concept of Mahdi in Twelver Shiʿism', in *Encyclopaedia Iranica*, ed. Ehsan Yarshater (http://www.iranicaonline.org/articles/islam-in-iran-vii-the-concept-of-mahdi-in-twelver-shiism).
14. Khuri, 'The Ulama', pp.304-5.

15. The term *mujtahid* was only used after Muḥaqqiq Najm al-Dīn Ḥillī (d. 676/1277) and Ibn al-Muṭahhar al-Ḥillī had incorporated the concept of *ijtihād*, which the early traditionists had rejected, into Imamite doctrine. See Rainer Brunner, 'Shi'ite Doctrine: Hierarchy in the Imamiyya', in *Encyclopaedia Iranica*, ed. Ehsan Yarshater (http://www.iranicaonline.org/articles/shiite-doctrine-ii-hierarchy-emamiya).
16. Brunner, 'Shi'ite Doctrine: Hierarchy in the Imamiyya'.
17. Khuri, 'The Ulama'.
18. Brunner, 'Shi'ite Doctrine: Hierarchy in the Imamiyya'.
19. Khuri, 'The Ulama', pp.292-93.
20. Ayotallah Khomeini, *Al-hukūmah al-islāmiyyah* (Beirut: Dar al-Tali'a, 1979), pp.94-5.
21. Brunner, 'Shi'ite Doctrine: Hierarchy in the Imamiyya'.
20. Charles Butterworth and Sana Abed-Kotob, "Ilm', in *The Oxford Encyclopedia of the Islamic World*, ed. John L. Esposito (Oxford: Oxford University Press, 2009).
23. Butterworth and Abed-Kotob, "Ilm'.
24. Ibn ʿAbd al-Barr, *Jāmiʿ bayān al-ʿilm*, ed. A.M. Uthman, 2 vols. (Madinah: Al-Maktabah al-Salafiyyah, 1968), vol.1, pp.12-13.
25. Muḥammad b. Idrīs al-Shāfiʿī, *Al-Risālah*, ed. A. M. Shākir (Cairo, 1940).
26. Butterworth and Abed-Kotob, "Ilm'.
27. Ḥasan b. Yūsuf b. al-Muṭahhar al-Ḥillī, *Mabādiʿ al-wuṣūl ilā ʿilm al-uṣūl* (Al-Najaf: n.p., 1970). Cited in Butterworth and Abed-Kotob, "Ilm'.
28. Butterworth and Abed-Kotob, "Ilm'.
29. Ibid., "Ilm'.
30. Oussama Arabi, *Studies in Modern Islamic Law and Jurisprudence* (Leiden: Brill, 2001), pp.27-28
31. Sayyid Sa'eed Akhtar Rizvi, *The Justice of God* (Dar-Es-Salaam: Bilal Muslim Mission of Tanzania, 1992), p.2.
32. Qur'anic verses 3:182, 8:51, 22:10, 10: 44 and 4:40
33. Mohammad Ali Shomali, *Discovering Shi'i Islam* (London: Centre for Cultural and Ethical Studies, 2010), p.48.
34. Shomali, *Discovering Shi'i Islam*, p.47.
35. Muhammad b. Ali b. Babawayh, *al-Tawhid* (Qom: Jamā'at al-Mudarrisin, 1995), p.362. Cited in Shomali, *Discovering Shi'i Islam*, p.47.
36. Hossein Modarressi, 'Rationalism and Traditionalism in Shī'ī Jurisprudence: A Preliminary Survey', *Studia Islamica* 59 (1984), pp.141-58.
37. Mohsen Kadivar, *Ḥaqq al-nās: Islām wa-ḥuqūq-i bashar* (Tehran: Kavir, 2008). Cited in Yasuyuki Matsunaga, 'Human Rights and New Jurisprudence in Mohsen Kadivar's Advocacy of New-Thinker Islam', *Die Welt des Islams* 51 (2011), p.363.
38. Butterworth and Abed-Kotob, "Ilm'.
39. Shomali, *Discovering Shi'i Islam*.
40. Abdolkarim Soroush, 'The Evolution and Devolution of Religious Knowledge', in *Liberal Islam: A Sourcebook*, ed. Charles Kurzman (Oxford: Oxford University Press, 1998); Nasr Hamid Abu Zayd, *Reformation of Islamic Thought: A Critical Analysis* (Amsterdam: Amsterdam University Press, 2006).
41. Abu Zayd, *Reformation of Islamic Thought*.
42. *Ijtihād* means independent reasoning, and its derivative *mujtahid* is recognized as a

scholar who is competent in interpreting the law. See Aron Zysow, 'Ejtehād', in *Encyclopaedia Iranica*, ed. Ehsan Yarshater (http://www.iranicaonline.org/articles/ejtehad).

43. Ḥasan b. Yūsuf b. al-Muṭahhar al-Ḥillī, *Mabādiʿ al-wuṣūl ilā ʿilm al-uṣūl* (Tehran, n.p., 1892), p.51.

44. Modarressi, 'Rationalism and Traditionalism in Shīʿī Jurisprudence', p.149.

45. Moojan Momen, *An Introduction to Shi'i Islam: The History and Doctrine of Twelver Shiism* (New Haven, CT: Yale University Press, 1985), pp.184-207.

46. Muhammad Iqbal, *The Reconstruction of Religious Thought in Islam,* (Kitab Bhavan, 2000).

47. Suha Taji–Farouki (ed.), *Modern Muslim Intellectuals and the Qur'an, (*New York: Oxford University Press, 2004).

48. amina wadud, *Qur'an and Women* (New York: Oxford University Press, 1999).

49. Kecia Ali, *Sexual Ethics & Islam: Feminist Reflections on Qur'an, Hadith and Jurisprudence* (Oxford: Oneworld, 2006).

50. Kadivar, *Ḥaqq al-nās*. Cited in Matsunaga, 'Human Rights and New Jurisprudence', p.366.

51. Kadivar, *Ḥaqq al-nās*. Cited in Matsunaga, 'Human Rights and New Jurisprudence'.

52. Matsunaga, 'Human Rights and New Jurisprudence', pp.358-381.

53. Abdolkarim Soroush's writings are cited in Ziba Mir-Hosseini, 'Religious Modernists and the "Woman Question": Challenges and Complicities', in *Twenty Years of Islamic Revolution: Political and Social Transition in Iran since 1979*, ed. Eric Hooglund (Syracuse, NY: Syracuse University Press, 2002), pp.74-95.

54. Judith E. Tucker, *Women, Family, and Gender in Islamic Law* (Cambridge: Cambridge University Press, 2008).

55. Abdal Hakim Murad, 'Islam, Irigaray, and the Retrieval of Gender', April 1999, (http://www.masud.co.uk/ISLAM/ahm/gender.htm).

56. Mohammad Solokolaei, *Hekmat'haye tafavot-e ghesas-e zan va mard* (Qom: Samaneye Nashriyat, 2006).

57. Javadi Amoli, Muhammad Abd al-Munim Khaqani Abd Allah and Abd al-Muttlib Ridza, *Tasnīm fī tafsīr al-qur'ān* (Qom: Dar al-Isra, 2010).

58. Kadivar, *Ḥaqq al-nās*, p.115.

59. Kadivar, *Ḥaqq al-nās*, p.370.

60. 'Ali Akbar Kalantari, *Hukm-i thanawiyyah dar tashri'-i islami*, cited in Matsunaga, 'Human Rights and New Jurisprudence', p.370.

61. Kadivar, *Haqq al-nās,* p.128.

62. 'Voices of a New *Ijtihad*', in 'Who Speaks for Islam? Who Speaks for the West?', conference at New York University Center for Dialogues: Islamic World-U.S.-The West, February 10-11, 2006.

63. Ziba Mir-Hosseini, 'Sharia and National Laws in Iran', in *Sharia Incorporated: A Comparative Overview of Legal Systems in Twelve Muslim Countries in Past and Present*, ed. Jan Michiel Otto (Leiden: Leiden University Press, 2010), pp.341.

64. Matsunaga, 'Human Rights and New Jurisprudence'.

65. Mir-Hosseini, 'Sharia and National Laws of Iran'.

66. Zaki al-Milad, 'Dynamic Jurisprudence and Women's Activism', *Shabakeye IranZanan*, January 9 2010, (http://www.iranzanan.com/first_point/002200.php).

67. Al-Milad, 'Dynamic Jurisprudence and Women's Activism'.

68. Matsunaga, 'Human Rights and New Jurisprudence', p.358.

69. Al-Milad, 'Dynamic Jurisprudence and Women's Activism'.
70. Fazlur Rahman, *Revival and Reform in Islam*, ed. Ebrahim Moosa (Oxford: Oneworld, 1999); Ronald Nettler, 'Mohamed Talbi's Ideas on Islam and Politics: A Conception of Islam for the Modern World', in *Islam and Modernity*, eds. J. Cooper, R. Nettler and M. Mahmoud (New York: I. B. Tauris, 2000), p.131.
71. 'Voices of a New *Ijtihad*'.
72. Sayyid Mohsen Saidzadeh, 'Fiqh and Fiqahat', *UCLA Journal of Islamic & Near Eastern Law* 1(2) (2002), pp.239, 240–41, 246–47. Cited in Shadi Mokhtari, 'The Search for Human Rights within an Islamic Framework in Iran', *The Muslim World*, 94 (2004), pp.469-79.
73. Mokhtari, 'The Search for Human Rights within an Islamic Framework in Iran'.
74. Qur'anic verse 2:185.
75. Amira Sonbol, 'The Genesis of Family Law: How "shari'ah", Custom and Colonial Laws Influenced the Development of Personal Status Codes', in *Wanted: Equality and Justice in the Muslim Family*, ed. Zainah Anwar (Selangor: Musawah, 2009), pp.179-203.
76. Qur'anic verses 9:70, 10:44, 29:40 and 30:9.
77. Qur'anic verses 58:11 and 2:259.
78. Al-Sharīf al-Raḍī, *Nahj al-Balagha*, trans. Sayed Ali Reza (Rome: European Islamic Cultural Center, 1984), p.204.
79. Hamid Mavani, 'Paradigm Shift in Twelver Shi'i Legal Theory (*uṣūl al-fiqh*): Ayatullah Yusef Saanei', *The Muslim World* 99(2) (2009), pp.335-55.
80. Yusef Saanei, *Qaymumat-e mader* (Qom: Mu'assasah-ye Farhangi-ye Fiqh-e Thaqalayn, 2005), pp.55-56, as cited in Mavani, 'Paradigm Shift in Twelver Shi'i Legal Theory (*uṣūl al-fiqh*)'.
81. Yusef Saanei, *Berabari-ye diyah* (Qom: Mu'assasah-ye Farhangi-ye Fiqh-e Thaqalayn, 2005), pp.9–12, as cited in Mavani, 'Paradigm Shift in Twelver Shi'i Legal Theory (*uṣūl al-fiqh*)'.
82. Arabi, *Studies in Modern Islamic Law and Jurisprudence*, pp.27-8; Mavani, 'Paradigm Shift in Twelver Shi'i Legal Theory (*uṣūl al-fiqh*)'.
83. Mir-Hosseini, 'Sharia and National Laws in Iran'.
84. Mir-Hosseini, 'Sharia and National Laws in Iran'.
85. Mavani, 'Paradigm Shift in Twelver Shi'i Legal Theory, (*uṣūl al-fiqh*)'.
86. Ibid., 'Paradigm Shift'.
87. Ibid., 'Paradigm Shift'.

Bibliography

Abu Zayd, Nasr Hamid, *Reformation of Islamic Thought: A Critical Analysis* (Amsterdam: Amsterdam University Press, 2006).

Afsaruddin, Asma, *Excellence and Precedence: Medieval Islamic Discourse on Legitimate Leadership* (Leiden: Brill. 2002).

___, 'The Epistemology of Excellence: Sunni-Shi'i Dialectics on Legitimate Leadership', in *Speaking for Islam: Religious Authorities in Muslim Societies*, eds. Gudrun Krämer and Sabine Schmidtke (Leiden: Brill, 2006), p.49.

___, 'Authority, religious', in *Encyclopedia of Islam, Three*, eds. Gudrun Krämer, Denis Matringe, John Nawas, Everett Rowson, (Leiden: Brill, 2011).

Ali, Kecia, *Sexual Ethics & Islam: Feminist Reflections on Qur'an, Hadith and Jurisprudence* (Oxford: Oneworld, 2006).

Amir-Moezzi, Mohammad Ali, 'Islam in Iran vii. The concept of Mahdi in Twelver Shiᶜism', in *Encyclopaedia Iranica*, ed. Ehsan Yarshater, (http://www.iranicaonline.org/articles/islam-in-iran-vii-the-concept-of-mahdi-in-twelver-shiism).

Amoli, Javadi, Muhammad Abd al-Munim Khaqani Abd Allah and Abd al-Muttlib Ridza, *Tasnīm fī tafsīr al-qur'ān* (Qom: Dar al-Isra, 2010).

Arabi, Oussama, *Studies in Modern Islamic Law and Jurisprudence* (Leiden: Brill, 2001).

Brunner, Rainer, 'Shi'ite Doctrine: Hierarchy in the Imamiyya', in *Encyclopaedia Iranica*, ed. Ehsan Yarshater, (http://www.iranicaonline.org/articles/shiite-doctrine-ii-hierarchy-emamiya).

Butterworth, Charles and Sana Abed-Kotob, "ᶜIlm', in *The Oxford Encyclopedia of the Islamic World*, ed. John L. Esposito, (Oxford: Oxford University Press, 2009).

al-Ḥillī, Ḥasan b. Yūsuf b. al-Muṭahhar, *Mabādiᶜ al-wuṣūl ilā ᶜilm al-uṣūl* (Tehran, n.p., 1892).

—, *Mabādiᶜ al-wuṣūl ilā ᶜilm al-uṣūl* (Al-Najaf: n.p., 1970).

Ibn ᶜAbd al-Barr, *Jāmiᶜ bayān al-ᶜilm*, ed. A.M. Uthman, 2 vols. (Madinah: Al-Maktabah al-Salafiyyah, 1968).

Ibn Babawayh, Muhammad b. Ali, *al-Tawhid* (Qom: Jamā 'at al-Mudarrisin, 1995).

Iqbal, Muhammad, *The Reconstruction of Religious Thought in Islam* (Kitab Bhavan, 2000).

Kadi, Wadad, 'Authority', in *Encyclopedia of the Qur'ān*, ed. Jane Dammen McAuliffe, (Leiden: Brill, 2001-6).

Kadivar, Mohsen, *Ḥaqq al-nās: Islām wa-ḥuqūq-i bashar* (Tehran: Kavir, 2008).

Khomeini, Ayotallah, *Al-hukūmah al-islāmiyyah* (Beirut: Dar al-Tali'a, 1979).

Khuri, Foud, 'The Ulama: A Comparative Study of Sunni and Shi'a Religious Officials', *Middle Eastern Studies* 23(3) (1987), pp.291-312.

Matsunaga, Yasuyuki, 'Human Rights and New Jurisprudence in Mohsen Kadivar's Advocacy of New-Thinker Islam', *Die Welt des Islams* 51 (2011), pp.358-81.

Mavani, Hamid, 'Paradigm Shift in Twelver Shi'i Legal Theory (*uṣūl al-fiqh*): Ayatullah Yusef Saanei', *The Muslim World* 99(2) (2009), pp.335-55.

Al-Milad, Zaki, 'Dynamic Jurisprudence and Women's Activism', *Shabakeye IranZanan*, January 9 2010, (http://www.iranzanan.com/first_point/002200.php).

Mir-Hosseini, Ziba, 'Religious Modernists and the "Woman Question": Challenges and Complicities', in *Twenty Years of Islamic Revolution: Political and Social Transition in Iran since 1979*, ed. Eric Hooglund, (Syracuse, NY: Syracuse University Press, 2002, pp.74-95).

—, 'Sharia and National Laws in Iran', in *Sharia Incorporated: A Comparative Overview of Legal Systems in Twelve Muslim Countries in Past and Present*, ed. Jan Michiel Otto, (Leiden: Leiden University Press, 2010).

Modarressi, Hossein, 'Rationalism and Traditionalism in Shī'ī Jurisprudence: A Preliminary Survey', *Studia Islamica* 59 (1984), pp.141-58.

Mokhtari, Shadi, 'The Search for Human Rights within an Islamic Framework in Iran', *The Muslim World*, 94 (2004), pp.469-79.

Momen, Moojan, *An Introduction to Shi'i Islam: The History and Doctrine of Twelver Shi'ism* (New Haven, CT: Yale University Press, 1985).

Nettler, Ronald, 'Mohamed Talbi's Ideas on Islam and Politics: A Conception of Islam for the Modern World', in *Islam and Modernity*, eds. J. Cooper, R. Nettler and M. Mahmoud, (New York: I. B. Tauris, 2000).

al-Raḍī, al-Sharīf, *Nahj al-Balagha*, trans. Sayed Ali Reza. Rome: European Islamic Cultural Center, 1984.

Rahman, Fazlur, *Revival and Reform in Islam*, ed. Ebrahim Moosa (Oxford: Oneworld, 1999).

Rizvi, Sayyid Sa'eed Akhtar, *The Justice of God* (Dar-Es-Salaam: Bilal Muslim Mission of Tanzania, 1992).

Saidzadeh, Sayyid Mohsen, 'Fiqh and Fiqahat', *UCLA Journal of Islamic & Near Eastern Law* 1(2) (2002).

Saanei, Yusef, *Berabari-ye diyah* (Qom: Mu'assasah-ye Farhangi-ye Fiqh-e Thaqalayn, 2005).

___, *Qaymumat-e mader* (Qom: Mu'assasah-ye Farhangi-ye Fiqh-e Thaqalayn, 2005).

al-Shāfiʿī, Muḥammad b. Idrīs, *al-Risālah*, ed. A. M. Shākir, (Cairo, n.p. 1940).

Shomali, Mohammad Ali, *Discovering Shi'i Islam* (London: Centre for Cultural and Ethical Studies, 2010).

Solokolaei, Mohammad, *Hekmat'haye tafavot-e ghesas-e zan va mard* (Qom: Samaneye Nashriyat, 2006).

Sonbol, Amira, 'The Genesis of Family Law: How "shari'ah", Custom and Colonial Laws Influenced the Development of Personal Status Codes', in *Wanted: Equality and Justice in the Muslim Family*, ed. Zainah Anwar, (Selangor: Musawah, 2009, pp.179-203).

Soroush, Abdolkarim, 'The Evolution and Devolution of Religious Knowledge', in *Liberal Islam: A Sourcebook*, ed. Charles Kurzman, (Oxford: Oxford University Press, 1998).

Taji-Farouki, Suha (ed.), *Modern Muslim Intellectuals and the Qur'an* (New York: Oxford University Press, 2004).

Tucker, Judith E., *Women, Family, and Gender in Islamic Law* (Cambridge: Cambridge University Press, 2008).

wadud, amina, *Qur'an and Women* (New York: Oxford University Press. 1999).

Zysow, Aron, 'Ejtehād', in *Encyclopaedia Iranica*, ed. Ehsan Yarshater, (http://www.iranica-online.org/articles/ejtehad).

5

Okawa Shumei's and Toshihiko Izutsu's Islamic Studies and its Implications for Understanding Justice

Xiaofei Tu

Introduction

In this chapter, I intend to address three related questions: First, why have Japanese scholars been interested in Islamic studies? Given that Japan is geographically far removed from the Islamic world and that there are few Muslims living in Japan, the answer is far from self-evident. Second, how have Japanese scholars approached Islamic studies? Not surprisingly, the methodologies of Japanese studies of Islam have been drastically different from Western methods. Third, how should we assess Japanese approaches in the European languages (especially English) dominated academic world? I present two prominent Japanese scholars of Islam, Okawa Shumei and Izutsu Toshihiko, as case studies. I argue that the answers to these two questions lie in the political and spiritual justice that Japanese thinkers have long advocated. Before I proceed to my main argument, I will provide a contextual introduction to Japan's interaction with Islamic thought, as it is unlikely to be familiar to readers.

Okawa Shumei's Islamic Studies in the Context of Japanese Pan-Asianism

My first case study is Okawa Shumei (1886-1957), a pioneer of Islamic studies in Japan. More than 40 years ago, Takeuchi Yoshimi, a prominent literary critic and scholar of Islamic studies in his early years, lamented about the lack of scholarly interest in Okawa Shumei.[1] This sentiment was understandable given the fact Okawa has commonly been labelled as an ultra-nationalist and right-winger, and was tried (although not convicted) after WWII as the only civilian Class A War Criminal by the International Military Tribunal for the Far East. Things have changed since then and studies of Okawa's thought have mushroomed and his work has gained the attention of more prominent scholars, including Bunzo Hashikawa and Takehiro Otsuka. In the meantime, there has been a surge of interest in Islam and the Islamic world in Japan since the synchronized terrorist attacks on the United States in 2001. Against this background, it is of academic and political importance to revisit Okawa's scholarship on Islam in the light of his critique of Western imperialism, because it still holds contemporary relevance, as will be discussed below.

Most existing scholarship, however, focuses on Okawa's thought and political activities in his later life and leaves his formative years untouched. This chapter will begin with Okawa's intellectual growth in his late teens to early twenties, especially his exposure to Christianity, a monotheistic Abrahamic tradition that fundamentally changed the young Okawa's trajectory of thinking. In this regard, Okawa's diaries dating from 1903 to 1921 in his *Collected Works* are most helpful sources.[2] However, before delving into Okawa's intellectual world, it is necessary for us to understand the social and intellectual backdrop from which Okawa's thought emerged.

The modern period in Japan began in 1853 when Commodore Matthew C. Perry, the commander of the East Asia squadron of the American Navy, first sailed his so-called Black Ships into Tokyo Bay off the strategic harbor of Uraga. Carrying a letter from then President Millard Fillmore demanding free trade, Perry's fleet easily defeated the resistance of the local Japanese warriors armed with traditional samurai swords and the old Bushido spirit. Later, a Japanese Shogun who was subdued by the superior American military power laid the entire blame on a local military leader Taki Zenzaburo. The latter's commitment of hara-kiri, the Japanese custom of self-immolation and honorable suicide, greatly impressed the Westerners who witnessed the event.[3]

The acceptance of Perry's ships was an event that had no precedent in Japan's history. As a result of this shock, the Tokugawa feudal system that had endured for some 260 years began to collapse. The realization of the commencing of a new age of colonialism had been unique and central to the modern Japanese psyche. Facing Western colonialism, Japanese intellectuals such as Sato Kaoru (1815-1852) stated that it is proved that the Western imperialists had no shame or propriety. They considered only their own interests and did not care whether others lived or died. Nevertheless, he conceded that it was natural that different countries had different customs, and it was theoretically impossible to determine whose custom was right, neither was there a basis to condemn the law of the jungle.

The discovery of a powerful and foreign world forced unprecedented changes on the Japanese. On March 14 1868, the Japanese Emperor, escorted by his ministers, paid worship to Heaven, Earth, the gods and the imperial ancestors. After the solemn ceremony, a royal decree was announced that Japan would be, among other things, seeking knowledge of the outside world. With that, Japan – in the philosopher Nishitani Keiji's expression – stepped onto "the stage of world history."[4] On one level, in the eyes of the Japanese, the European colonial powers represented a military force backed by modern industry. This motivated Japan to call for its citizens to enrich the country and strengthen the military, which was fulfilled within a short span of time. At a deeper level, the West was seen as representing civilization and enlightenment. Implicitly or even explicitly, Japan and Asia in general saw themselves in a state of barbaric pre-civilization. Thus, a craze to imitate Western thought and culture took place.

However, such a colossal change was destined to bring about confusion and turmoil. The advocates of rapid westernization clashed with traditionalists who hung on to old ideas and lifestyle. Samurai rebels, for example, ignited by the desire for political reforms, clashed with government troops armed with imported western armory in 1877, as clumsily portrayed in the Hollywood blockbuster *The Last Samurai*. In the meantime, despite Japan's effort to come in line with the mainstream global community, world events had never ceased to provide reasons to stimulate new rounds of nationalistic fervor. For instance, the 1924 US immigration law that restricted Asian immigrants caused the Japanese an indelible sense of humiliation and sparked calls for defense of Asian pride.

The Japanese intelligentsia responded to these gargantuan changes in different ways. On the one hand there were radical modernizers who admired Western civilization to the extent that they mimicked every aspect of the Western lifestyle. Instead of the old diet of fish, they preferred to devour "the civilized meat" – beef. Mori Arinori, a senior Japanese statesman, encouraged Japanese people to marry Westerners. Inoue Kaoru claimed that Japan should be changed into a "European country". As the Minister of Foreign Affairs, he built with public funds the notorious European-style club Deer Park (1883) for Japanese high society to "modernize" its social life. Extravagant masquerade parties were thrown there to entertain local and foreign dignitaries. (Curiously enough, this embodiment of Western luxury was named "Deer Park," after a famous line in the Chinese classic *Book of Odes*. This naming alone is enough to signal the contradictions of modernity and tradition in nineteenth-century Japan.) Later on, this landmark building, along with all the activities associated with it, was attacked by Japanese nationalists as a financial waste and a sign of capitulation to the West. Inoue answered them, stating that in order for the Westerners to treat the Japanese as equals, the Japanese should act like their equals, including in their everyday lives. Inoue's theory did not bear out as the Western powers declined to change the unequal treaties with Japan – a major ambition of Inoue in his capacity as the Foreign Minister – and Inoue lost face and had to resign.[5]

The apparently desperate, even ludicrous, attempts to catch up with the West were intended to follow the footsteps of Western modernization as closely as possible: rationalization, separation of state and church, a free market economy, urbanization, and promotion of individual rights. The lack of time to digest these changes meant the modern world was difficult for the Japanese to cope with; while the foreign origin of the modernization incited hostility in the general public toward foreigners. As such, it proved to be a hotbed for an equally strong counter-movement of cultural nostalgia that in turn fostered a rabid political and cultural nationalism.

Not everyone in Japan, however, was dazzled by the attractions of the West. Kakuzo Tenshin advocated an Asian spirituality that was supposedly superior to Western materialism and could serve as a corrective to the latter. In *The Ideals of the East*, Kakuzo claimed that Asia was one in spirit.[6] From the perspective of civilizational comparison, Kakuzo considered Asia a homogeneous and harmonious unity, which included "Arabic chivalry, Persian poetry, Chinese ethics, and Indian philosophy." Islam was said to be "Confucianism on horseback."[7] The reason Kakuzo associated Islam with Confucianism was because he saw in Islam both a collective moral code and idyllic elements akin to those born from the Yellow River in China. He then contrasted this peaceful, tolerant, coexisting ethos of the East to the aggression and invasion of the West. Kakuzo believed that savagery meant that humans were bound by their pursuit of material needs while civilization meant the overcoming of physical desires with morality. The simple life of Asia did not need to feel ashamed when compared to the material luxury of the West.

Not surprisingly, the young Okawa and his generation were caught in the confusion between fascination with the West and the calling of his own tradition. Incidentally, in 1903 when Okawa began writing his diaries, Huchimura Misao, a high school student, committed suicide and attracted national attention. In the last letter he left, Huchimura stated that the reason for his suicide was his realization of the insignificance of the individual life in the face of a gigantic and meaningless world. "Endless time, infinite space, what is this five-foot body of mine doing within that space and time? All I can say about the world is: I do not understand." The untimely death drew tears from people of all walks of life, and a few youths were inspired by Huchimura and followed his example. Iwanami Shigeo (1881-1946), the later founder of Iwanami Publishing House, was one of the young admirers of the suicide. "I know there is no better place than the realm of death, I have not killed myself only because I lack the courage."[8]

Traditional Japanese society and family had provided an order and value to the world. This order might be hierarchical or even authoritarian, but it had given the individual the duty to cooperate with, and the promise of help from, societal and family members. Hence the individual possessed a sense of belonging. This order, however, was broken in the process of modernization. In addition to sociological factors, there was a more serious cultural dislocation and disorientation following the introduction of Western values. The donkey in Buridan's dilemma could not decide between two heaps of grass and finally died of hunger.[9] Similarly, competing values threaten to leave people with confoundedness and spiritual starvation. A more appropriate parallel would be Karl Jasper's "boundary situation": the anxieties built into the structure of human existence are occasioned by the predicaments of suffering and fate.[10] When the shelters of traditional beliefs crumble, the existential predicaments become extremely acute. Takeshi Umehara shrewdly remarked: "We did not accept the Christian God, but killed our own gods (Buddhism and Confucianism)".[11] The "plentitude" and conflictions of the spiritual claims made to modern Japanese people contributed to their spiritual paucity and pronounced lack of existential solutions.

In addition, social issues were being redefined with new value paradigms. Poverty is as old as human history; however, it came to be widely recognized as a "social problem" in Japanese society in the middle of the Meiji era (1868-1912). In the traditional Buddhist worldview, poverty was seen as resulting from the bad karma of the individuals who suffer from it. It was in modern times that poverty became recast as an issue demanding social and political remedies. The beginning of socialism in Japan is closely associated with the introduction of monotheistic religions. In 1898, a group of Japanese Protestants denounced the Biblical miracles and the doctrine of the Trinity as "unscientific" but advocated social justice for the poor and oppressed in the spirit of Christian teachings. Many of them later became founding members of the Japanese Social Democratic Party. In Japan, socialism did not begin as a movement of the poor, but as the cause of middle class intellectuals recognizing the suffering of people with whom they had no direct relationship.

When he was a third-year student in Middle School, Okawa went to the local Tsuruoka Roman Catholic Church for the purpose of studying European languages. He appreciated the religious atmosphere at the church but did not become a Christian. There are three reasons for this. First, Okawa was unsatisfied with the church ecclesiastics and rituals. In his diary, Okawa talked about how he was not impressed by the ornate decorations in the church. The long Catholic service reminded him of boring Buddhist rituals. Second, he was turned off by the irrational elements in Christian beliefs such as miracles. Again, in his diaries, Okawa wrote that Jesus's message rather than doctrines of the Trinity and Resurrection are the pillars of Christian religion. Religious miracles are to him *bagarashi* (stupid). Third, he believed that Christianity is preoccupied with otherworldly concerns and does not do enough about injustice in this world. Sarcastically, he pointed out the contrast between a priest preaching spirituality at the pulpit and the offering plate passed around in the pews. When he asked the priest why good people suffer and the evil prosper, the priest gave him the ordinary answer that this life is but a test; eternal rewards and punishments are waiting in the next life. Okawa was not persuaded. For him, spiritual messages without efforts to change the social system were hypercritical. Indeed, justice is an enduring concern for Okawa in his life. Thus, Okawa believed that he needed to transcend Christianity as an institutionalized religion in order to seek the essence of all religions.[12]

Okawa went on to college at Tokyo University. In 1910, Okawa published with his pen name "Shirokawa Ryotaro" his first essay on Islam, a general introduction to the Islamic religion. At this time, Okawa did not know Arabic and his main source on Islam was Max Muller's translation and studies. Not unlike his educated contemporaries, Okawa's interest in religion was primarily about a direct experience with the transcendent that is stripped of external rituals and institutional hierarchy. For him, the experience of the transcendent in Islam is not so different from Buddhist experience of the so-called Buddha nature, as both are direct contact with the ultimate reality.

A turning point in Okawa's life occurred when he saw a book in a bookstore about British colonialism in India. The terrible sufferings of the Indian people and the atrocities committed by the Western colonizers made a major impression on him. It was at this time that he developed the idea of Asian unity.[13] At a later date he joined the South Manchurian Railway Company, under its East Asian Research Bureau, in order to put his political ideas into action. Together with another famous political activist, Ikki Kita, Okawa founded the nationalist political group Yūzonsha. In the 1920s, he became an instructor of history and colonial policy at Takushoku University, where he was also active in the creation of anti-capitalist and nationalist student groups.

It is worth noting that Okawa's attitude towards war had gone through major changes. In his youth Okawa had been strongly anti-war due to his conviction that war destroys human lives. However, that quickly changed when the Russo-Japanese war broke out over the control of East Asia in 1904. In his diary Okawa wrote: "we should treat fellow human beings with respect and love, little birds with a protective instinct, but lions and wolves with violence."[14] When the bombing of Pearl Harbor occurred, Okawa revealed that it was an auspicious day in human history. Alluding to resistance led by the Hojo generals against the Mongol invasion back in thirteenth century, he said when the Mongols came from the North, Japan had Hojo (*ho* means north in Japanese) to fight them; now when the enemy was the Americans coming from the East, Japan has Tojo (the wartime prime minister; *to* means east in Japanese) to fight them. For Okawa, this was not a coincidence but providence.[15]

After WWII, the Allies prosecuted Okawa as a Class-A War Criminal. Of the twenty-eight people with this charge, he was the only one who was not a military officer or government official. The Allies described him to the press as the "Japanese Goebbels" and claimed that he had long agitated for a war between Japan and the West. In return, Okawa did not recognize the court's authority, repeatedly calling it a show trial and a comedy. During the trial he behaved eccentrically: speaking in German and other foreign languages, and claiming he was an American military officer in charge of the prison. Okawa was transferred from the jail to a US Army hospital in Japan, which concluded that he had mental instability. Later, he was transferred to the Tokyo Metropolitan Matsuzawa Hospital, a famous mental hospital, where he completed the first Japanese translation of the entire Holy Qur'an. He was released from hospital in 1948 and spent the final years of his life writing a memoir, *The Gate to Peace and Joy*, reflecting on how he found peace and joy in confinement.[16] In October 1957, the prime minister of India, Jawaharlal Nehru, requested an audience with him during a brief visit to Japan. The invitation was hand-delivered to Okawa's house by an Indian Embassy official, who found that Okawa was already on his deathbed and was unable to leave the house. This episode, among others, suggests that Okawa was a significant figure until the end of his life.

In scholarly terms, Okawa's knowledge in Islamic doctrines per se did not reach the level of an expert. For instance, he had to enlist the help of German and English translations of Qur'an in order to translate it into Japanese. However, the importance of Okawa's work lies in the fact that he personified the pre-war Japanese interest in Islam for both spiritual and political reasons. In the early part of the twentieth century, facing the Russian and the British military presence in the Middle East, Japan, as a regional power and an emerging world power, felt compelled to make its presence felt. In the meantime, leaders and intellectuals in the Muslim world were also interested in the success story of Japan's modernization. In 1938, the semi-governmental Institute for the Study of the Islamic World was founded, sponsored by important political figures such as Tokugawa Iemasa, a member of the Japanese aristocracy and the Japanese ambassador to Germany. Members of the Institute included well-known scholars Toshihiko Izutsu and Yoshimi Takeuchi. In order to justify Asian unity, they and Okawa advocated a theory that nations are not defined by blood, language, religion or culture, but by the common experience of oppression by Western imperialism.[17]

Philosophically, many prewar Japanese thinkers drew upon Hegelianism. In the early twentieth century, Hegelianism was not only respected in Europe but also dominant in North America and Asia. Based on Hegelian historical dialectics, the Japanese considered their time a crucial point in human history. In Hegelian terms, the historic "thesis" is the premodern era when different cultures and civilizations were isolated from each other and co-existed relatively peacefully. The "antithesis" is the defeat of Islam at the hand of European powers starting in late medieval times that marked the end of world peace and the rise of Western imperialism. Finally, the twentieth century is the "synthesis" when imperialism would be destroyed and world peace restored. These scholars of Islam believed that Japan's actions in fighting Western imperialism would not only shape the fate of Japanese people but change forever the course of the entire human race.[18]

Moreover, what drew Okawa to monotheism and Islam in particular is the latter's concept of theodicy. For Okawa, divine justice should be represented on both individual and national levels. It is the reason that he stressed the importance of justice in the international arena. To him, the grave injustice of his time was not only unfair economic distribution among individuals or social classes but political and economic inequality among nations. He observed that the European colonial powers had enslaved people in Asia and the rest of the world. Therefore, on the principle of justice, he argued that it is legitimate and righteous for Asian people, including Muslims and the Japanese, to force the aggressors out. Okawa rejected the traditional Western concept that Islam had killed its way to control a large part of the world. He acknowledged that although military force played a part in the earlier history of Islam, nevertheless it was due to the power of its spiritual message that Islam has spread over the globe. For instance, Okawa compared the evangelism of Christianity and Islam in North Africa. Despite the huge resources that the Christian missions spent there, Islam had been more successful in winning people's hearts and minds in this region.[19] Citing the Western image that Islam is a religion with the Qur'an in one hand and the sword in the other, Okawa turned the stereotype on its head by saying that spiritual traditions and military weapons are both necessary for the self-defense of the Asian peoples. He used this rationale to support Japan's action in the Pacific war.

The reality of surrender at the end of WWII shattered Japan's dream of changing the course of human history. However, the question of Western dominance and international injustice remained. In postwar Japan, people continued to wrestle with the question of whether their country should wholeheartedly embrace the West or stand up to the latter's military and economic dominance. Some who oppose Western cultures and capitalism have tried other alternatives. For instance, the former Islamic studies scholar Takeuchi Yoshimi turned his attention to socialist China as a more realistic model than Islam for Japan. The left-leaning journalist Soichiro Tahara, a towering figure in mainstream Japanese media, wrote an influential book on Okawa and other prewar Pan-Asianist thinkers.[20] Even in contemporary times, critiques of modern-day capitalism and neoliberalism continue to reference him for intellectual resources.[21]

Toshihiko Izutsu's Islamic Studies and the Question of Comparative Philosophy

My second case study is Toshihiko Izutsu (1914-1993), an intellectual historian who had a dominant influence in Islamic studies in Japan and an important place in contemporary English-language scholarship on Islam. The main writings of Toshihiko Izutsu included a new Japanese translation of the Qur'an, influential works in Qur'anic studies, the history of Islamic thought, as well as comparative philosophy of religion. It is no exaggeration to say that most contemporary Japanese intellectuals depend on the work of Izutsu to understand Islam.

His two books, *The Structure of the Ethical Terms in the Koran: A Study in Semantics*, published in 1959 (revised as *Ethico-Religious Concepts in the Qur'ān* in 1966) and *God and Man in the Koran, Semantics of the Koranic Weltanschauung*, published in 1964 are ground-breaking works in Qur'anic studies, and have been translated into Arabic, Persian, and Turkish. The mainstream Qur'anic studies in the West are primarily historical, making use of Arabic commentaries and chronicles, as well as pre-Islamic Jewish and Christian sources. On the other hand, Muslim Qur'anic studies are mainly exegetical, heavily relying on traditional commentaries and biographical literature. In addition, Muslim study of the Qur'an is dominated by verse-by-verse and word-by-word commentaries, sometimes missing a holistic grasp of the whole structure of the holy text. Izutsu's studies broke new ground in Qur'anic studies in that he undertook a semantic analysis of the interconnection of key terms in the Qur'an. By so doing, Izutsu attempted to help readers appreciate its underlying Weltanschauung or worldview. Izutsu's approach has influenced both Muslim scholars and non-Muslim scholars in the field.[22]

Here worldview refers to the ways in which people conceptualize and interpret the world that surrounds them. In semantic analysis, a word has a "basic" meaning as well as "relational" meanings. Basic meaning is the original meaning attached to the word. On the other hand, relational meanings of a word are manifestations of the spirit of a language and faithful reflections of the collective psyche of the people who speak this language. Thus, vocabulary is not a homogenous plane but a multi-strata structure formed linguistically by groups of "semantic fields."[23] We can logically infer from Izutsu that, by examining key "ethico-religious" terms in Islam and other spiritual traditions, we are able to understand the basic structures of meaning through which we understand ourselves and the world, including our sense of justice.

For instance, capitalism, socialism and Islam may all agree on the concept of "justice", yet each have a different interpretation of what justice is. Capitalism defines justice in terms of individual interest. Socialism considers individual interest subordinate to collective interest. Finally, Islam considers envisions justice as a condition under which the individual is not dominated by society and vice versa.[24]

Beyond his Qur'anic studies, Izutsu had a high regard for Islamic theology, especially its mysticism. This propensity to mysticism came from his personal and scholarly experience. In his youth, his father trained him rigorously in Buddhist meditation. In Izutsu's own words, his father "forced" him to learn meticulous meditative techniques:

> First, write the Japanese word "mind" in black ink with a brush. Gaze at the word for a certain time, then tear off the paper and visualize the same word. The mind should be focused on the word day and night without stopping. Next, forget the word "mind" but try to find the mind itself. Finally, forget the word, the mind and the self altogether in order to be united with nothingness.[25]

This is a typical traditional Zen training, in which concepts are initially utilized and eventually abandoned on the path to the ultimate truth. In real life, Zen teachings and practice were the usual topics of the Izutsu family's father-son conversation. Although Izutsu's father was a businessman, not a Buddhist priest or a man of letters, this early training paved the way for Izutsu's life career. Later, Izutsu was also exposed to ancient Greek mystical thought. When reading the pre-Socrates thinkers, Izutsu felt as if he was hypnotized. The words of the early thinkers seemed to sound themselves out loudly and there was a mystic aura surrounding the books. In Izutsu's words, it was a cosmic experience in which the *logos* was revealed. Such *vita contemplativa* is the utmost happiness one can ever achieve on earth.

Izutsu does not conceal his scholarly preferences. In his *History of Islamic Thought*, he uses only five pages to discuss the Shariᶜah while devoting 323 pages to mysticism.[26] While recognizing the utmost importance of the Shariᶜah in Islamic faith and life, Izutsu effectively excludes it from intellectual history. He quotes an anecdote that when the philosopher Ibn Rushd died, his body was carried on one side of a donkey to be taken back to his home in Morocco. To balance out the weight, all the books that he had written were put on the other side. Upon seeing this, his contemporary Ibn ᶜArabī lamented the futility of knowledge – bookish knowledge was the equivalent of a corpse. In contrasting the rationalism of Ibn Rushd and the mysticism of Ibn ᶜArabī, Izutsu favors the latter.[27] For Izutsu, rationalization, institutionalization and politicization ossify the living religious spirit. In contrast, mysticism is a living force within religions and the antidote to ossification. Izutsu himself is aware of the danger that while his elevation of the mystical aspects of Islam might appeal to Japanese readers, there could be resistance among practicing Muslims who faithfully follow the Shariᶜah. He understands the sensitive nature of the issue but insists on his approach because his ultimate goal is a *philosophia perennis* that answers to universal human existential concerns.

For instance, there is a common thread in all religions about human impermanence. In Arabic literature, time is variously described as merciless tyrant and a wild animal that bites with sharp teeth. No sooner does a way of living seem enjoyable to us, then time destroys it completely whether it be old or new. Poets lament: "The daughters of time have shot at me from a place I cannot see; what can man do when he is shot at without being able to shoot back?" and "indeed time always gains ultimate victory; even talismans are of no use against the destructive power of time."[28] We could easily draw parallels with Buddhism and Taoism where life is compared to a short dream or the passing shadow of a racing horse. There cannot be human answers to this question. In Islam as well as in Buddhism and Taoism, God and his justice can only console humans, though these traditions may perceive God differently.

In his *Sufism and Taoism*, Izutsu attempts to prove that the philosophical structures of both systems are dominated by the unity of existence. Here unity is formed by many different things. Thus, the world of being is represented as a kind of ontological tension between unity on the fundamental level (*ḥaqq* for Ibn ʿArabī and Tao in Taoism) and multiplicity on the commonsensical level. All the things that constitute multiplicity are, after all, different phenomenal forms assumed by the Absolute in a process of self-manifestation.

Izutsu emphasizes the boundless mercy of God shown to the creatures in Islamic mysticism. For Ibn ʿArabī, the mercy of God extends to everything actual and possible. Divine mercy is an ontological fact radically different from the human feeling of compassion in that it has nothing to do with human judgments and valuation. This ontological mercy makes things exist. In other words, God gives existence to everything. At the same time, the God of the Qur'an is the God of justice. He shows unlimited love and compassion, yet also inflicts punishment upon those who refuse to obey him. For Ibn ʿArabī, however, God's wrath is subordinate to his love. Mercy precedes wrath. Indeed, exercise of divine mercy is nothing other than the process of the self-manifestation of the Absolute. God's mercy covers the entire world of beings: it is a gratuitous gift that is absolutely impartial and indiscriminating. Some things are good and others are bad only in terms of human beings' subjective and relative point of view. Properly speaking, however, everything without exception is good. Even human obedience and disobedience to God are ultimately two aspects of one and the same thing. When Moses threw down his staff in the presence of Pharaoh, the staff turned into a snake. It is a play on words in Arabic (staff/rebellious and snake/life)[29] and a symbolic act in which rebellion against God is turned into spiritual life resulting from obeying Him. All events that occur and all actions that are taken are without exception due to the divine will and, in this sense, there can be no distinction between good and bad or right and wrong.[30] Similarly, in Taoism, good and evil, beauty and ugliness, are all self-manifestation of the Absolute.

The impartiality of God/the Absolute demands us to rethink our understanding of equality. In current Western discourses, equality is often narrowly understood in economic, legal, and political senses. While each of these is important in its own right, Izutsu reminds us not to forget that the ultimate equality is the equality for human beings as creatures in front of God. We share common longings for God's mercy across national, ethnic, and political boundaries that are human, temporal, and in the final analysis, unimportant. For Izutsu, religion is the experience of a total response to the total being of the ultimate reality, while religious doctrine, fellowship, and ritual are secondary "expressions" in thought and action of this fundamental experience. Moreover, this experience of reality in the final analysis is mystical beyond the scope of reason and logic. Finally, this religious experience, or at least the potential for it, is universal and innate in all human beings. Thus, it is possible for one to understand the religiosity in radically different forms of religion than one's own. Indeed, precisely because linguistical and cultural expressions are not translatable and in the final analysis inadequate, ultimate truth is only found in the mystical experience beyond the named.

Izutsu makes it clear that he is not interested in philosophy on paper; rather he studies philosophy for the sake of life. This could fittingly be called a philosopher's existential concerns. According to Steven Collins, "existential concern" means "an intellectualist attempt to find a reflective, rationalized ordering of life and death as a conceptual and imaginary whole, and to prescribe some means of definitive (if only imaginatively, so far as a non-believer can tell) escaping suffering and death."[31] Emanuel Levinas remarked that humans have two ways to access the outside world, namely, by vision and by contact. Thus, in our language, we metaphorically say that we "see" or "grasp" the truth. We find an example of the philosophy of vision in Plato when he compared the human world to an arena. In this parable, there are three groups of people in the arena. The least worthy people are the peddlers who hawk their goods and try to make a profit. Better than the first group are the athletes competing for prizes and honor. But the worthiest among all people are the spectators who observe and reflect without participating. In real life, similarly, the least worthy are the profiteers. Better than them are people who lead an active life, such as politicians. The best people for Plato, however, are the philosophers who observe life without active participation. On the other hand, we could argue that Japanese thinkers have a philosophy of contact: they are always in contact with human life and its concerns. The Confucian and Buddhist practitioners seek a total commitment and are expected to attain an intellectual and spiritual transformation. The goal for Confucians is "to combine the unfathomable truth with daily life." In Buddhism, theories that cannot be put into practice are considered a mere "play of words" (*prapanca*) and pure philosophical speculation does not serve a soteriological purpose. Izutsu identifies with this "oriental approach," and bluntly stated that he had no interest whatsoever in "objective" studies of religion that do not concern human existence.[32]

Conclusion

The central place of justice in Islamic theology does not go unnoticed in Okawa and Izutsu's Islamic studies. Furthermore, the work of both provides fresh perspectives for us to understand justice. For Okawa, the application of the concept of justice in today's world serves as an unequivocal protest against, and a possible corrective to, Western materialistic, worldly values. It is interesting to compare Okawa's thought with the philosophy of nonviolence that is supposed to be quintessentially "Asian" in Western media and political discourse. In a much-distorted version of the philosophy of nonviolence, past wrongs committed by colonial and imperial powers are covertly erased and an arbitrary closure imposed on the victims. It is a perhaps well-intended but nevertheless unwise gesture that advises people not to look back at their history. However, there is an inevitable sense of guilt for the offenders, past and present, in the face of transcendent justice. In the Western public panic about terrorism, for example, one senses an unconscious exposure of people's collective guilt.

On the other hand, a lesson from Izutsu is the reality and importance of universal religiosity in all human beings. I believe a new term is needed to convey this important concept and I shall call it "spiritual justice." By spirituality, I mean the attempt, based on beliefs in a transcendence that cannot be reduced to possible materialistic, political or ideological interpretations, to address human existential concerns, as defined above. On the other hand, while in our time the term "justice" has been applied to many areas and probably stretched thin, to my knowledge, not many people have used the combination of the two words "spiritual" and "justice" in the sense that I mean it.

Scholars like John Caputo, Charles Taylor and Talal Asad have all questioned secularist biases in philosophical and ethical discussions, namely, the totalizing effects of disembodied reason and the normative regime of the rational subject. In various ways, the works of Durkheim, Freud and Marx have given impetus to this secularist narrative in modern times.[33] Taylor pointed out that both religious beliefs and rational propositions of unbelief are necessarily conditioned by our embeddedness in language and culture, which are "ahead of" any rational decisions. William Connolly is disappointed that secularist immodesty and prejudices unfairly rejected "a set of orientations to reverence, ethics, and public life that deserve to be heard."[34] I find Izutsu's position is in line with that of Taylor and Connolly in that they all agree our ethical considerations, including consideration for justice, must be rooted in our spiritual traditions.

Islamic teachings and Izutsu's interpretation of them make clear that human beings are more than biological entities and that they long for more than material possessions. As Fichte aptly put it, human beings are not animals on all fours, constantly looking downward for food. There are hope, faith, and love on the human horizon. We solemnly acknowledge that humans are equal in the most comprehensive meaning of the word. That is, humans are equal not simply because we all need to be physically fed and sheltered but also because all of us equally need to be spiritually comforted. Moreover, as Izutsu pointed out above, while Allah's justice is omnipresent beyond any doubt, it also has a dimension that transcends human understanding. The lesson is that divine justice cannot be tied down or pigeonholed within specific political ideologies or actions. For instance, a "materialistic" interpretation of Islamophobia as caused by the West's economic interest in the oil-rich Middle East seems to be inadequate in that it misses the opportunity to look at the social ills in our contemporary secularist society and to heed what Islam has to say about them. It seems to me that the same materialistic approach is a slight to Islam as comprising important spiritual teachings and disguises it as something else (in the above example, competition for natural resources).

As scholars of religion (including scholars of Islam), we should not shy away from scholarship's "practical" purpose, that is, to fulfill people's spiritual needs. As we see in the example of Izutsu, comparative religion can serve as a route to spirituality in an age when the appeal of institutionalized religion has waned. If the objective study of religions should be understood as not to favor any particular religion, it does not mean to forbid the existence of a spiritual dimension in our studies. As the scholar of religion Wach put it: "To me there is something pathetic about the modern historian of religion who uses strong words only when he tries to persuade his reader that he has no conviction."[35] For Izutsu, comparative religions is a much-needed tool for people in modern times to grasp the universal nature of the "incurable" religious quest innate to all human beings. This understanding has important implications for our appreciation of the concept of justice. After all, if we are sincere when professing our belief in Islam or other time-honored world traditions, the ultimate justice can only be understood and realized in the final universal salvation promised by them.[36] Thus, we can conclude that Izutsu's study of Islam is both "horizontal" in placing other religions in a comparative perspective and "vertical" as a spiritualized, uplifting view of life and the world.

Endnotes

1. Yoshimi Takeuchi (竹内好), 大川周明のアジア研究 竹内好全集 (Tokyo: 筑摩書房, 1980), p.177.
2. Shumei Okawa (大川 周明), *Collected Works* (大川周明集) (Tokyo: 筑摩書房, 1961).
3. A. B. Mitford, *Tales of Old Japan: Folklore, Fairy Tales, Ghost Stories and Legends of the Samurai* (Dover Publications, 2005).
4. Keiji Nishitani (西谷 啓治),世界觀と國家觀 (Tokyo: 弘文堂書房, 1943).
5. Jielin Xu (许介鳞), 近代日本論 (台北:故鄉, 1987), p.37.
6. Kakuzo Okakura (岡倉 覚三), *Ideals of the East: The Spirit of Japanese Art* (New York: E. P. Dutton and Company, 1920).
7. Okakura, *Ideals of the East*, pp.3-4.
8. Yong Li (李永), 日本近代思想论 (On Modern Japanese Thought) (台北: 牧童出版社, 1975), pp.349-50.
9. Jack Zupko, *John Buridan: Portrait of a Fourteenth-Century Arts Master* (Notre Dame, IN: University of Notre Dame Press, 2003), p.258.
10. Quoted in Hao Chang, 'New Confucianism and Contemporary China', in *The Limits of Change*, ed. Charlotte Furth (Cambridge: Harvard University Press, 1976), p.279.
11. Umehara Takeshi, 'Heidegger and Buddhism', *Philosophy East and West* 20(3) (1970), p.171.
12. Okawa, *Collected Works*, vol.1, p.108.
13. Shumei Okawa (大川 周明), *A History of Anglo-American Aggression in East Asia* (Tokyo: 大東亜出版, 1944).
14. Quoted in Masuke Kudo (工藤 真輔), 思想形成期の大川周明：宗教と社会主義. 北大法学研究科ジュニア・リサーチ・ジャーナル, 15 (2008), p.38.
15. Okawa, *Collected Works*, vol.2, p.727.
16. Seicho Matsumoto (松本清張), 砂の審廷：小說東京裁判 (Tokyo: 筑摩書房, 2008).
17. Yoshimi Takeuchi (竹内好), 顧頡剛と回教徒問題, 竹内好全集 (Tokyo: 筑摩書房, 1981), pp.212
18. Yoshimi Takeuchi (竹内好), 大川周明のアジア研究, 大川周明集 (Tokyo: 筑摩書房, 1975), p.405; Nohara Shiro, 回教圏研究所の思い出, 野原四郎 アジアの歴史と思想 所収 (Tokyo: 弘文堂書房, 1966), pp.88-89. See also Takeuchi Yoshimi (竹内好), *What Is Modernity?: Writings of Takeuchi Yoshimi* (New York: Columbia University Press, 2005), p.103ff.
19. Okawa, *Collected Works*, vol.1, p.290.

20. Soichiro Tahara (田原 総一朗), 日本近現代史の「裏の主役」たち 北一輝, 大川周明、頭山満, 松井石根……「アジア主義者」の夢と挫折 (PHP 研究所, 2013).

21. Nakatani Iwao, テロとクーデターの時代「五-一五事件 大川周明訊問調書」を読み解く (第2回) 黄金大名をはびこらせた新自由主義の欺瞞, *Monthly Nippon* 13(2) (2009).

22. Masataka Takeshita, 'Toshihiko Izutsu's Contribution to Islamic Studies', *Journal of International Philosophy* 7 (2016), pp.78-81.

23. Toshihiko Izutsu (井筒俊彦), *God and Man in the Koran: Semantics of the Koranic Weltanschauung* (Tokyo: The Keio Institute of Cultural and Linguistic Studies, 1964), pp.18-20.

24. Mohamed Aslam Haneef and Hafas Furqani, 'Developing the Ethical Foundations of Islamic Economics: Benefitting from Toshihiko Izutsu', *Intellectual Discourse* 17(2) (2009), p.176.

25. Toshihiko Izutsu (井筒俊彦), *Collected Works* (井筒俊彦著作集) (Tokyo: 中央公論社, 1991), p.198.

26. Izutsu, *Collected Works*.

27. Izutsu, *Collected Works*, p.332.

28. Izutsu, *God and Man in the Koran*, p.124.

29. In Arabic, staff is ʿ*āṣan* and rebellious ʿ*āṣin*, while snake is *ḥayyah* and life *ḥayāt*.

30. Toshihiko Izutsu(井筒俊彦), *Sufism and Taoism: A Comparative Study of Key Philosophical Concepts* (Berkeley: University of California Press, 1983), p.116.

31. Steven Collins, *Nirvana and Other Buddhist Felicities* (Cambridge: Cambridge University Press, 1998).

32. Izutsu, *Collected Works*, p.336.

33. Edwin Ng, *Buddhism and Cultural Studies* (Burwood, Australia: Palgrave-Macmillan, 2016), p.3.

34. Quoted in Ng, *Buddhism and Cultural Studies*, p.5.

35. Wach Joachim, *Sociology of Religion* (Chicago: University of Chicago Press, 1944), p.10.

36. Izutsu, *God and Man in the Koran*, p.234.

Bibliography

Chang, Hao, 'New Confucianism and Contemporary China', in *The Limits of Change*, ed. Charlotte Furth, (Cambridge: Harvard University Press, 1976).

Collins, Steven, *Nirvana and Other Buddhist Felicities* (Cambridge: Cambridge University Press, 1998).

Haneef, Mohamed Aslam and Hafas Furqani, 'Developing the Ethical Foundations of Islamic Economics: Benefitting from Toshihiko Izutsu', *Intellectual Discourse* 17(2) (2009), pp.173-99.

Iwao, Nakatani, テロとクーデターの時代「五-一五事件 大川周明訊問調書」を読み解く(第 2 回) 黄金大名をはびこらせた新自由主義の欺瞞, *Monthly Nippon* 13(2) (2009).

Izutsu, Toshihiko (井筒俊彦), *The Structure of Oriental Philosophy: Collected Papers of the Eranos Conference* (Tokyo: 慶応義塾大学出版会, 2008).

___, *The Concept of Belief in Islamic Theology* (Kuala Lumpur: Islamic Book Trust, 2006).

___, *Ethico-religious Concepts in the Qur'ān* (Ithaca, NY: McGill-Queen's University Press, 2002).

——, *Collected Works* (井筒俊彦著作集) (Tokyo: 中央公論社, 1991).
——, *Sufism and Taoism: A Comparative Study of Key Philosophical Concepts* (Berkeley: University of California Press, 1983).
——, *God and Man in the Koran: Semantics of the Koranic Weltanschauung* (Tokyo: The Keio Institute of Cultural and Linguistic Studies, 1964).
Kudo, Masuke (工藤 真輔), 思想形成期の大川周明：宗教と社会主義. 北大法学研究科ジュニア・リサーチ・ジャーナル, 15 (2008), pp.27-48.
Li, Yong (李永), 日本近代思想论 (*On Modern Japanese Thought*). 台北: 牧童出版社, 1975.
Matsumoto, Seicho (松本清張), 砂の審廷：小說東京裁判 (Tokyo: 筑摩書房, 2008).
Mitford, A. B., *Tales of Old Japan: Folklore, Fairy Tales, Ghost Stories and Legends of the Samurai* (Dover Publications, 2005).
Nishitani, Keiji (西谷 啓治), 世界觀と國家觀 (Tokyo: 弘文堂書房, 1943).
Nohara, Shiro (野原四郎), 回教圏研究所の思い出, 野原四郎 アジアの歴史と思想 所収. 弘文堂, 1966.
Okakura, Kakuzo (岡倉 覚三), *Ideals of the East: The Spirit of Japanese Art* (New York: E. P. Dutton and Company, 1920).
Okawa, Shumei (大川 周明), *Collected Works* (大川周明集) (Tokyo: 筑摩書房, 1961).
——, *A History of Anglo-American Aggression in East Asia* (Tokyo: 大東亜出版, 1944).
Tahara, Soichiro (田原 総一朗), 日本近現代史の「裏の主役」たち 北一輝, 大川周明、頭山満, 松井石根……「アジア主義者」の夢と挫折. PHP 研究所, 2013.
Takeshita, Masataka, 'Toshihiko Izutsu's Contribution to Islamic Studies', *Journal of International Philosophy* 7 (2016), pp.78-81.
Takeuchi, Yoshimi (竹内好), *What Is Modernity?: Writings of Takeuchi Yoshimi* (New York: Columbia University Press, 2005).
——, 顧頡剛と回教徒問題, 竹内好全集, 14 vols. Tokyo: 筑摩書房, 1981.
——, 大川周明のアジア研究 竹内好全集 第八巻. Tokyo: 筑摩書房, 1980.
——, 大川周明のアジア研究, 大川周明集. Tokyo: 筑摩書房, 1975.
Umehara, Takeshi, 'Heidegger and Buddhism', *Philosophy East and West* 20(3) 1970, pp.271-81.
Xu, Jielin. (许介鳞), 近代日本論. 台北:故鄉, 1987.
Zupko, Jack, *John Buridan: Portrait of a Fourteenth-Century Arts Master* (Notre Dame, IN: University of Notre Dame Press, 2003).

Index